ENGLAND SPEAKS

THE MACMILLAN COMPANY
NEW YORK · BOSTON · CHICAGO
DALLAS · ATLANTA · SAN FRANCISCO

MACMILLAN AND CO., LIMITED
LONDON · BOMBAY · CALCUTTA
MADRAS · MELBOURNE

**THE MACMILLAN COMPANY
OF CANADA, LIMITED**
TORONTO

England Speaks

A Symposium

By

A. P. HERBERT
A. A. MILNE
E. M. FORSTER
DR. A. S. DUNCAN-JONES
RONALD KNOX
J. R. CLYNES
C. E. M. JOAD
HAROLD LASKI

NEW YORK
THE MACMILLAN COMPANY
1941

PRINTED IN THE UNITED STATES OF AMERICA
AMERICAN BOOK—STRATFORD PRESS, INC., NEW YORK

PUBLISHER'S NOTE

The eight sections of this book were originally published separately as The Macmillan War Pamphlets. The distinguished character of their authorship and their success in their original form has prompted the publisher to produce them in this more permanent style.

CONTENTS

LET THERE BE LIBERTY

By

A. P. HERBERT

LET THERE BE LIBERTY

(A speech delivered at Bath)

I HAVE never pretended to be a full-fledged politician ready to spread my wings anywhere in the vast spaces of public affairs. If anyone had any burning questions in his heart concerning agriculture, the Gold Standard, the price of butter or the management of industry, it would be no use putting them to me. Nor shall I, in this address, attempt to explain to the Allied War Staffs how to win the war. But I think it may be useful to say something about certain general questions of which I do pretend to have some knowledge, and to examine them rather more closely than the pukka politician, rightly preoccupied with problems of detail, has time to do; and I have taken for my subject "Our Liberties", a phrase which is often used but seldom examined.

Some of those liberties are in abeyance under the Emergency Powers Act, and more may be before very long, but the special powers Parliament has given Parliament can take away, and my theme is not affected by those busy three hours of Parliamentary business on May 22, when we all lent our lives and property to His Majesty's Government. For years after the last war most of us complained about D.O.R.A.; it was aggravating, for example, not to be able to buy chocolates in a theatre after eight o'clock, and I wrote a good deal on the subject myself. But the irritation that so small a vexation caused shows how strongly we returned to the notion of liberty after the enemy had been defeated. When a German is heard to complain that he still, under an old decree of the Third Reich, cannot visit a beer garden between certain hours, we shall know there is liberty again in Germany.

We see and hear some surprising things in the present war; and that is just as well, for life would be drab indeed if we could predict or govern the course of events to the point of eliminating surprise. I am surprised to hear it said that here and there are people, and peoples, who are luke-warm about the present war. I have met very few luke-warmers myself—I am not quite sure that I have met any. Our people are not, like the young Prussians, always click-ing their heels, waving their arms, saluting, shouting, or singing dreary ditties about dubious characters like the late Horst Wessel. But it would be a great mistake to suppose that they are not as dogged, determined and undauntable as they have ever been.

Twenty-five Years Ago

Still, there may be more lukewarmers than I suppose; and if so, I cannot understand it. Twenty-five years ago I was a young man in His Majesty's infantry forces, and after six months in the ranks, I was just about to sail for the Dardanelles. In those days we had no doubt that we were justly engaged in a just war, which had been thrust upon us by an aggressive enemy, by our treaty obligations and our sense of duty. But I cannot remember that there was in our minds the same sense of urgency, of inevitability of life and death, of black and white, as must surely be present in our minds to-day. In 1914 we fought because our country was at war with another civilised country, and we should have presumed that she was right if we had not been certain of it. To-day we fight because the devil is abroad, because the Powers of Darkness are challenging mankind, because a spiritual pestilence is walking the world, because a great grease-spot is swiftly spreading over the map of Europe.

If we had been defeated in 1914, we should, at least, have gone down to a nation more or less like-minded with ourselves—a nation with which we had much sympathy and kinship. She had been, she was, a fruitful mother to the arts, to music, to literature and learning and science. She had much to show us and much to teach us in the making and the management of the things of the mind. There was even, in some ways, more liberty than we could show. Music and the arts were encouraged and subsidised and provided cheaply for the people; and some of us used to say lightly that at least under Germany we should get better beer whenever we wanted it. There was freedom of thought, and of worship, in spite of all the heel-clicking and heiling. A Catholic could worship in peace—a Jew could make fine music, write books or cure disease. To-day all that is at an end. Since the rule of Hitler began, not one work of merit in art or music has come from there. Germany has blown out her own brains and stamped upon her soul.

And that is not all. If Germany had defeated us in 1914 it would still have been possible for many thousands of our people to say that, apart from a patriotic preference for winning, they would not themselves have been much affected in their daily lives. That would have been true, in a sense, and up to a point. We must remember, and especially those who say that all war is futile—including the last war—that that war did fix the standard of life for this country, and other countries, at least for a generation. But, apart from bread and butter, from work and wages, it would have been true. That Germany, the Germany we defeated, was led by Prussia, arrogant, greedy and aggressive, but it had not yet turned barbarous and pagan, it had not made cruelty its favourite instrument, and brute force its only god. But to-day every single soul in every country that comes under the German heel knows what to expect. He is to expect that not merely in matters of work and wages will his life be altered and ordered by aliens, but in every moment of the day; that he will never speak without permission, never think without anxiety, nor go to sleep without fear. That is the fate designed for us and every other country on which the Führer sets his feet: and in such a struggle can anyone be lukewarm?

Slavery or Freedom?

I can well understand how a man in this country long unemployed might have said bitterly twelve months ago, "In Germany there are no unemployed", though, as somebody has well remarked, "There are no unemployed in Dartmoor Prison". I can understand such a man saying, only a few months ago, "What use is political liberty to me if I can't get work?" But if since then he has read only a little of what has happened in Austria, Poland and Czechoslovakia—and not to Jews only—he will agree to-day, I think, that he would much rather be poor but free in England, with all her faults, than busy in bondage under Prussian rule. He may not agree with me; and if not, it would be impertinent of me to argue with him. But certainly for 99 per cent. of mankind, rich, poor or middling, not only here but in every country in the world, the question in this war is not, "Do you like the Germans better than the English?", not "Do you believe in Parliaments?", not "Do you approve of the Treaty of Versailles?", but "Would you rather see Slavery or Freedom win?" That is the question not only for you and me and the unemployed, but for all those terrified neutrals and non-belligerents.

The Real Empire

And, whatever our dyspeptic moderns may think of the British Empire, I would say the same concerning the millions of every race and creed who, though they may not have full self-government, are still, like you and me, free subjects of the Crown. We, as the Germans are fond of pointing out, have conquered a corner or two of this planet. But what is our method when we have conquered? We do not stamp out the local faith, the local culture, the local customs, and impose our own upon the people by force. We do not command that Mahommedan mosques shall be designed by the British Prime Minister and built in the British style, or forbid the Hindu to worship as he will. We persecute no man because of his race or religion. We may regard ourselves as a superior race; but we do not on that account think ourselves entitled to destroy, or even to drive out, the others. We do not take the leading citizens and put them against a wall in order to break the spirit of the people. On the contrary, it has always been our way to encourage the people to live their own life, under their own leaders, traditions and faith, and to impose nothing upon them but what is necessary for the common safety, prosperity or health. Then, by degrees—and this is no idle talk, for it is happening every day—we approach the final goal, and we admit them, with all necessary precaution, to the dubious privilege, the difficult task, of governing themselves.

All this long process is complete, and indeed is ancient history, in the great Dominions. It is going slowly forward at this moment in India; and that it goes slowly is not a sign that we do not practise what we preach, that we do not really believe in liberty. Quite the contrary. It means that we are not going to hand over the reins of authority until we are sure that by so doing we shall not endanger the freedom of certain minorities.

Jungle Ballot

And if anyone still thinks that I am talking nonsense, let him visit the lovely island of Ceylon, as I have been lucky enough to do two or three times. Ceylon has been described as "the brightest jewel in the Imperial Crown". And that kind of expression calls up the kind of picture that malignant enemies and ignorant Englishmen like to make much of. It suggests to the modern mind the worst that anyone can mean by the vague term "Imperialism". It suggests the Arabian Nights—a selfish and illiberal tyranny. But what are the facts? In Ceylon we have introduced self-government to a degree that many thought to be politically dangerous, a degree that is certainly contrary to the material interests of our own people. In Ceylon we have instituted Adult Suffrage, though enormous numbers of the people are quite illiterate, are governed at elections by religious considerations and vote accordingly. In Ceylon there is a Parliament; but we have so arranged affairs that it is now quite impossible for a European, that is for those whose industry and capital have built up the prosperity of the island, to obtain a seat. I do not say that you have there complete self-government; I will not say that all is absolutely smooth and easy—this is a Colony at the half-way stage, or a little beyond it; and many, as I have said, think that we may have gone too far. But it is a fine example of our methods; it is a brilliant illustration of the sincerity of our professions. At the risk of every material interest we have grafted on to the Gorgeous East the Committees of the West; we have set up in the jungle the hustings and the ballot box. Right or wrong, it is at least doubtful if Herr Hitler would have the courage or the kindness to do the same.

From Runnymede to Ceylon

And there is much more than that. The vote, as some say bitterly but truly, is by no means the infallible key to happiness. When I was last in Ceylon I heard of some recent trouble in the island. An Englishman, described as an "agitator", had made himself obnoxious to the authorities by, as the phrase is, "stirring up the natives". The Governor, the King's representative, ordered his arrest and deportation. But the man, whose name I have forgotten, appealed to the King's judges in Ceylon—Englishmen like the Governor. He applied, I think, for a writ of Habeas Corpus. The King's judges decided that the King's representative had exceeded his powers, and they ordered the man to be released. For what reason? Because this gentleman had not been treated in accordance with the principles and undertakings laid down in Magna Carta, in the year 1215. I got hold of the judgments and read them carefully; and no man with any spark of imagination could have failed, I think, to feel, as I did, a thrill of pride and wonder—to sit in that tropical heat, among the fireflies and the flame-trees, 7,000 miles from London, and to realise that of all those thousands of dusky Buddhists and

Mahommedans about me, most of whom could not speak a word of my own language or write a word of their own, every one had a right not merely to vote for his own representative in the Council but to go to the King's judges and say, "The Governor, the King's servant, is not dealing fairly with me: what is more, he has broken the promises made to all the King's subjects by King John at Runnymede 700 years ago".

There is the reality of freedom; and there, I believe, is a true picture of the British Empire.

I recall a more amusing example. An appeal some years ago came up to the Judicial Committee of the Privy Council in London from some far corner of the Empire. The dispute, in the first instance, had been decided in a somewhat primitive manner, according to our notions, by the tribal chiefs, or witch-doctors; I think that there was some element of trial by ordeal—the litigants had to prove the justice of their case by walking unhurt over red-hot coals and so on. The plaintiff, not being satisfied with the result, appealed to a higher court, and was successful. But the case climbed on and up in the normal way through successive courts of appeal and it came at last to the Judicial Committee of the King's Privy Council which sits at Whitehall. And there four or five of the King's greatest judges solemnly decided that the witch-doctors had been right all the time, and the judgment of that primitive court was restored.

"With None to Make Them Afraid"

Now it might be said against us that such proceedings were a waste of time and money. But we are at least entitled to set them against the technique of Hitler and Co.

in dealing with the troubles of subject races. They are the kind of thing to bear in mind when you hear the malignant or the ignorant scornfully using against us the new insult "Imperialism". It is very easy, but quite untrue, to speak of the Empire as an area of servitude lashed to London by dividends and tribute. The truth is, as anyone could show, that the chain of British liberty and justice is → the real link, and that chain runs firm and continuous from the King in London to the most distant, the most backward of his domains.

Indeed, perhaps the best answer to the "anti-Imperialist" is to be found in some words that were used by King George V in 1935:

"In these days when fear and preparation for war are again astir in the world, let us be thankful that quiet government and peace prevail over so large a part of the earth's surface; and that under our flag of freedom so many millions eat their daily bread, in far distant lands and climates, with none to make them afraid."

"With none to make them afraid." This, then, as I see it, is the general issue which is joined, as the lawyers say, in this conflict. A victory for Hitler would mean the spread of despotism and darkness: the victory of the Allies will mean the survival and the spread of light and liberty not in Europe only, but wherever the sons of Adam dwell. I do not see how anyone can confess himself lukewarm or dubious in such a struggle.

The Great Divide

But let us examine a little more closely what we mean by "Our Liberties"—that hard-worked phrase—at home.

It is worth while to do this, because, as I think Lord

Baldwin once remarked, "Freedom is so much a part of the air we breathe that we hardly notice it". A very just saying. Or, to put it less elegantly, our liberties are like our teeth. We forget the very existence of our teeth until we have toothache, and then we feel that if only we had no toothache the whole of life would be luminous and blissful. So true is this remark that we spend a great part of our liberties in finding fault with the others.

Well, what are they? They are our Free Parliament, Free Press, and Speech, Free Worship, and Fair Play (by which I mean, in the main, our system and tradition of justice).

These are all "institutions"; but they are founded, all of them, on a single principle—the notion that the individual is the unit of life, that every single human soul, rich and poor, black or white, has merit, has respect, has rights. And of each individual soul the State is not the master but the servant. That is the British doctrine: the doctrine you will find in Magna Carta: "To no man will we deny, to no man delay, to no man will we sell justice or right", but it is also the Christian doctrine—the doctrine that God considers even the sparrows—and it is held by many nations whose institutions are different from ours. It is the doctrine of the United States, whose constitution, I believe, begins, "All men are equal. . . ." But whether you call it British, American, Christian or pagan, it is fundamentally opposed to the doctrine of Nazi Germany, where the State is all and the individual is nothing, denied the right to speak or think except as he is ordered by the particular bullies who happen to be on top at any given moment. Here is the Great Spiritual Divide between the beasts of Berlin and the greater part of mankind.

It would be a great mistake to suppose that this spirit of liberty, this respect for the human soul, can only flourish under our own particular customs and institutions, and I do not suggest it. They may conceivably exist and struggle under dictatorship as under what we loosely call "democracy". But, in practice and in fact, we may say without undue boasting, that they have had their longest, strongest, and widest life in those parts of the world which have come under our command.

It is just possible, therefore, that there is some particular merit in our institutions. And I, for one, believe profoundly, and fiercely, that there is.

Parliament and Press

Take the first two I mentioned—Parliament and Press. I have the honour to belong to both: and the more I see of them the more I believe that they are worth preserving. I know, I think, everything that can be said against both; and I shall not pretend that they are formally perfect. Few things that are free, alive and natural are perfect. The great thing is that they are free, have growth and the power to breed. The Robot may be perfect, but it is dead. The formation and arrangement of the elephant is open to a good deal of criticism; and no doubt, if the critics were put to it, they might devise a much more handsome and logical quadruped. But it would not be an elephant, and might not survive.

This being a free country, we rightly permit criticism of Parliament and Press, as of everything else. But at the present time, when we are fighting for "Our Liberties", I wish that some of us could feel, if we do not show, a more positive affection for the great institutions which are the expression and the defence of freedom; I am sorry, in particular, that the relations between those two great sisters in the democratic family, Parliament and Press, are not more cordial and understanding. You know how it is. The same politician who cries that we must defend Free Speech is almost apoplectic when he speaks of the Press—and too often he makes no distinction between one organ and another of that vast and varied body. On the other hand, you may see an editorial article hotly defending "democracy", and a few columns away, equally hot attacks by other members of the staff on Parliament, its proceedings, and most of its members—not to mention those low fellows, the humorists, who regard the whole thing as the biggest jest in the world.

Nonsense in the News

Well, you know, it won't do. At least when we are fighting for our institutions, and those institutions are being not merely questioned but derided by our bitter enemies, we should try to understand and know them a little better than some of us seem to do. It may matter little what is said about the individual Member of Parliament. But the cumulative effect of nonsense, if it is never answered, may be strong.

And the nonsense of which I am thinking is never answered. My colleagues in the House of Commons are inclined to shrug their shoulders and remark that many of the accusations against them cancel each other out. Which is true. If we are serious we are dull and dreary: if we are witty we are frivolous. If we make a lot of speeches we are "always talking" ("Why don't they *do* something?"), and if we sit quiet and support the Government we are "miserable Yes Men!" If we let Bills go through without much argument we are neglecting our duties, and surrendering the people's liberties; and if we make a strong fight in Committee we are pettifogging or pin-pricking in order to "get publicity", or simply to annoy. If we go off to the country to speak to our constituents or hear what they have to say, we are told that we should have been "in our places" at Westminster; but if we remain stolidly at Westminster we are "seduced by the famous 'club facilities'," and it is said that we should be much better occupied getting among our constituents and hearing what is what from them.

Not long ago there was a great attack on "Question-Hour". This was said to be a waste of time and money. Most of the questions were about trifling things that could be settled privately—and so on. But the other day a "popular" paper came out with a great complaint that "Question" hour was not longer, since, in the opinion of the writer, it was the most valuable feature of Parliament. He did not say whether he wanted the hour extended to two hours, to three, or four. (I think myself that when Ministers are in charge of a war with a mad beast one hour a day is quite enough.) But the point is that those who throw the largest stones are never agreed about the target.

Then there are some who seem to suffer the delusion that a Member who is not continually popping up and asking questions or making speeches is not doing his duty. But it would be highly undesirable, and indeed impracticable, for all Members to exercise continually their rights of Free Speech. Some of the quiet Members who are never heard of are the best. I remember gratefully what fine service some of them did in the battle for the Marriage Bill—men who from first to last were never mentioned in the papers. They never made a speech (time being short, it would have been a pity if they had). But they could be relied on to turn up at eleven in the morning to provide a quorum in the Standing Committee and vote down the enemy. More, they would arrange private meetings, see and persuade important people, and generally spread the gospel and assist the cause. Quite unknown, but quite invaluable work.

Then there are the clever young newspaper-men who slip into the Gallery for the first time (as a *Daily* young man did the other day), count thirty-eight Members of Parliament in the Chamber and go away and write a song about it. The only thing they have proved, of course, is that they can count. This criticism rests upon the nonsensical notion (*a*) that the sole job and justification of an M.P. is to sit in the Chamber and make or listen to speeches: and (*b*) that all 615 M.P.'s, whatever is being debated or done, should always be "in their place" in the Chamber. If this were sound, the German Reichstag would be the ideal Parliament; for all the members turn up punctually at the same time or give no trouble to anyone.

From Cottage to Cabinet

Now, what, after all, is the big, the simple justification of Parliament and Press? That they are strong, permanent, sensitive, and on the whole truthful, mirrors—or if you will, conductors—of the thoughts and feelings of the people; that there is no subject so humble, with something to say, so small, that he cannot at last bring it to the attention of Parliament or Press—or both—and if need be, of the Prime Minister himself. Which brings me back to the doctrine I mentioned, that every individual matters.

Now, once you think of Parliament in that way—the clever journalists never do—not merely as a debating society or a law-making body, but as a conductor of thought and feeling from the cottage to the King's Government, you will begin to understand the system better, and you will perceive that most of the accusations are nonsense.

The principle works in two ways—big and small. It means not only that, as I have said, each humble subject, if he has a just cause and one that can be remedied, can bring it to the highest place privately or publicly: it means as well that every small trickle of opinion on national affairs can move along its own channel towards Whitehall and Westminster, and if there are enough converging trickles they may become a swelling stream that moves Ministers and mountains. And this is no idle talk. You hear much about the "long Parliamentary week-ends", about the comfortable smoke-room. But even these have place and merit in the working of the constitution. The House may adjourn on Fridays at 4 o'clock; and some Members may go off for those "week-ends" even earlier. But they go, very many of them, to more meetings, more speeches—to be listeners as well as talkers. On Mondays they are back with the opinions of the people, of the farmers, the Church, the miners, the fishermen. These may not always be shouted in the Chamber; but they are whispered in the smoking-rooms, the lobbies, in the upstairs Committees, in the Whips' rooms; and so, very quickly, they reach the Cabinet Room. Great organs of the Press, as you may have noticed, may shout for many months and not be noticed. I can remember one or two great occasions in my short time when the main current of feeling in the House has taken a strong new turn between Friday and Monday, mainly because the Members have been among the people.

What the People Think

Now, quite apart from liberty, think how such a system must make for the efficiency and strength of any Government that seeks to have the people behind it, as wise Governments must. The Prime Minister knows from day to day what the people are thinking. What can Hitler know of what his people are thinking? They dare not even tell each other. Indeed, I have seen it stated once or twice, in books and papers, that from time to time when Hitler has graciously desired to know what his people were thinking about some particular subject, he has had to send a special messenger round the country to visit the various Gauleiters and ask them—though for the reason I have given already, they are not much more likely to know the truth than he. What a confession of darkness! The Prime Minister does not have to send an ambassador to the Lord Lieutenant to find out what the people of Bath are thinking.

We read much about our muddles and scandals and deficiencies. It is a great thing that we should read about them, for thus they may be remedied. Do you suppose there are no muddles, scandals or deficiencies in Germany? Of course there are. But behind the screen of darkness and terror it may take much longer to detect and correct them. Here, as I have said, the humblest citizen may expose a private trouble or a public wrong in Parliament, the courts, or the Press, or all three, within twenty-four hours of its discovery. For most of our citizens can write, and all may write a reasonable letter of criticism without fear of arrest, imprisonment, and flogging. You may write to your Member—I do not recommend the practice, or I shall get into trouble. The Member may exercise his privilege and pass on the complaint to the Government Department concerned. Or he may approach the Minister privately—very likely in that much-discussed "smoking-room", where at least ninety per cent of the talk is "shop". If he is not satisfied, he may put down a question; and in certain circumstances he may raise a debate. You, if you are not satisfied, may make speeches against him, or write about him in the Press. You may vote against him at the next election. You may found a society to prosecute your cause, hold meetings about it, make speeches in the parks, take deputations to the House of Commons. You do not all, I am glad to say, choose to exercise all your rights; but there they are. It is good to know that they are there; and it is certain that not one of them would be yours under the dominion of Nazi Germany.

From the Strangers' Gallery

And now, if I have made clear my conception of the importance and the place of Parliament (quite apart from the making of laws) I should like you to come back to the Strangers' Gallery. You may look down, like the clever young man from the *Daily* and perceive with surprise that there are only forty members present out of the six hundred and fifteen. But there may be many good reasons for that. It may be early on Friday morning, when most of the Members are still answering piles of letters from perfect strangers, to which an answer is expected by return, or are on their way to do some service in their constituencies a long way away. We may have debated the particular subject so often that we can get no further, and know it. It may be a trivial debate which ought never to have begun. Mr. Smith has as much right to speak his mind as I have;

but there is no reason why all the others should sit and listen to us if we talk nonsense.

And they have very many other things to do. Though the Chamber seems a desert, the Palace of Westminster may be a beehive; and at every corner your troubles and opinions are flying in or receiving attention. To-day perhaps the Chamber talks about coal. We are not all there. But the field of public affairs is so vast that no one can pretend to cover it all. To-morrow's debate is about agriculture, and Mr. Smith is in the library, deep in books and papers, preparing a speech about that. Jones is drafting amendments to the Finance Bill, or questions about unemployment; Robinson is upstairs at a meeting of citizens interested in the Colonies, or receiving a deputation of pensioners, spinsters or poultry-farmers. Thompson, next-door, is at a Committee on Proportional Representation, or Canals, or Drainage, or Divorce. Innumerable Smiths, all over the place, are meeting constituents, traders, societies, mayors, members, it may be, of the Ceylon legislature or the Jamaican Government, studying their case, answering their letters, or badgering Ministers about their grievances. When those clever fellows drop into the Gallery (for the first time) and count their forty heads, there may be four hundred Members in the building, all busy. But my main purpose is not to defend individual Members from attack, but to persuade you to see our free Parliament as I do—not as a mere debating chamber where well-fed Members make laws and speeches, but as the central pyramid of all our liberties, to which fly, unmolested on the wings of freedom, the thoughts, the troubles, of all the British world. And when they come there, they are more free than ever.

What we do about them is, of course, another question.

But again, if you are not satisfied, you are free, in normal times, to throw us out. That is not technically true at present. Yet I believe that Parliament is still, and has been throughout the war, a true and sensitive reflector of the country. It has nudged, but it has not nagged. It has talked, but not too much. It has struck, I think, a difficult but admirable balance between reasonable freedom and foolish interference. It has been cheerful but not complacent, robust but not rancorous. In a word, it has been like the British people. And those who thought that in a life and death struggle with a ruthless despotic power we should be compelled, for sheer efficiency, to scrap our ancient machinery of freedom, shut up the "talking-shop", and put a muzzle on the people's representatives were making, I am sure, a very big mistake.

A Free Press

Much, very much, of what I have said, I would repeat about the British Press, though, with all deference to my colleagues, I believe that Parliament is the more sensitive and accurate reflector of the two. Few of us, I think, are as proud and grateful as we ought to be about the British Press. It is one of the blessings that we take for granted. Few of us realise the appalling special difficulties under which the papers labour at the present time—caught between the General's wife who complains each morning that "there is nothing in the papers" and the General who rages that there is far too much. Few of us perceive and acknowledge the concentrated skill and speed which bring the great papers to our breakfast every morning—well printed on expensive paper, full of instruction, encouragement and entertainment—and even, from time to time, a small patch of news. Few of us realise, when we rightly condemn the occasional naughtiness of this paper or the permanent naughtiness of that, the reticence and restraint which, in the face of great temptations, is maintained by the rest. In any large and spirited family there is likely to be a naughty child or two; and it is far better to have a spirited family than a troop of slaves. It is generally worth while to risk a little respectability, or even more, for the sake of freedom. Though let me add this: I am not lunatic about liberty; and where there is deliberate and persistent abuse of liberty I would curtail or suspend it without hesitation, that men may learn to value it better. But whatever you may think of this paper or that, the big point is this, every one of you can sit down to-night, even now when we are at war, and write to Fleet Street to say that he dislikes Mr. Churchill, that Parliament is full of unpatriotic, corrupt or senile Yes-men, that on the whole Communists are right, that Hitler is not as black as he is painted, or any other nonsense that may enter his head. And, if he chooses the right paper, he will see his nonsense printed. Hitler would say that this was madness. I think myself that it is good and glorious.

About freedom of worship, and free speech generally, I could say little that would not be obvious to you all.

To the Lukewarm

But in case there is anyone who is still lukewarm about "Our Liberties" or thinks that they are not worth fighting for, let him try to imagine a day without them. He wakes, a little anxiously, and sees the daylight with relief, for in the dead of any night the political police may invade his

home without warning, without warrant, without charge
or explanation. He finds, I suppose, a newspaper with his
breakfast or at the station; but every day there is nothing
in it but praise for his rulers and what they do, dictated by
the same rulers. It is no use for him to say, as every indignant Englishman may do, "I shall write to the papers
about it", for there is no paper that may print his accusation. In the train, in the office, in the street, he will not
speak his mind on any public affairs without glancing over
his shoulder and lowering his voice. At lunch-time, in the
restaurant, the notice "Do not discuss politics" hangs over
his table—not in war-time only but in peace. If it is a Sunday, he may go to his place of worship; but he cannot be
sure that the priest will not be in prison. At home every
book, every picture on the walls, every piece of music that
is played or sung, must conform to the pattern prescribed
by his political leader, and if he even sings the wrong song
he may be in for trouble. Even in the home, before his
oldest friends, before his own children, he is afraid to say
what he thinks. There are spies at the window, at the
back-door; he cannot trust his servants; his children may
give him away at school. If upon some charge, however
false, he is arrested, there is no Magna Carta to which he
can appeal, no writ of Habeas Corpus, no nonsense about
imprisonment without trial, about the right to be heard
by counsel. He is as helpless, as rightless, as a straw upon
the sea.

So the day passes—his body fed, maybe, his mind and
muscles occupied, his income adequate—but what a life!
And at the end of day there is perhaps the saddest, most
degrading scene of all. This man, this fine flower of centuries of civilisation, is permitted to know nothing of what

is being said and done outside his own country. He is the heir of centuries of scientific discovery: he has all the manifold and magical channels of modern communications at his disposal. Yet he is as remote, as ignorant of the world, as the savage in the jungle; for every channel is closed to him by his own paternal Government. And it is death to listen to what the world is saying. Yet at night, starving for knowledge, he determines to risk death for it. He turns on his wireless and allows to blare through a loud-speaker some crude patriotic speech or music. Then, clapping earphones to his ears and cowering in a cupboard or under the bedclothes, he listens, guilty and terrified, to the news of the world. And so to bed.

Such is the condition of darkness to which Herr Hitler has brought his people: such is the fate of all who fall under his "protection". We are last—or last but one—upon his list. But I am not going to press that point. It has become almost irrelevant. The time has gone by when any given country could say properly, "Am I concerned in, or endangered by this affair? If not, I will keep out of it". All countries that are, or were, part of the healthy civilised order of things are concerned in this; because the whole of that order is threatened by the German pestilence. It is no longer nation against nation—it is black against white—the devil against God—or what you will. Who, if I am right, can be lukewarm in such a struggle? There never should have been a neutral in this war, and, sooner or later, there will be none. But we cannot expect the unhappy, ill-defended neutrals to come in with us so long as there is a single sign of flabbiness or doubt among us. Let us expel them both. Those of us who can find no fun in war can surely at least find fire for this one. We do not fight for dividends or domination, we fight against the powers of darkness. We are in the van of those who say, "Let there be liberty. Let there be light". And we are entitled to use once more the words of John Milton: "Methinks I see in my mind a noble and puissant nation, rousing herself like a strong man after sleep, and shaking her invincible locks."

WAR WITH HONOUR

By

A. A. MILNE

WAR WITH HONOUR

"PRENDERGAST rose from the body. 'Poison,' he said briefly. 'One of the barbituric group.' I remembered suddenly the Brown-Smiley case.[1]" And at the bottom of the page the irrelevant observation "[1]*The Brown-Smiley Case* (Pump. 7s. 6d.)."

Like most readers of detective stories, I have resented this method of self-advertisement which I am now to practise. My apology is that the practice is forced on me by the scope and intention of this pamphlet. For it is an epilogue to a book called *Peace with Honour* which I wrote in 1933–34, and it is addressed primarily, but not exclusively, to readers of that book. That is to say, it is addressed to Pacifists by a Pacifist. I do not think that I could possibly write of this war without referring to what I have already written about War; and I must take the risk that some of you may seek further reference at your own expense. The risk is a small one, and my personal profit negligible.

"Peace with Honour"

I wrote *Peace with Honour: An Enquiry into the War Convention* as an ordinary man who hated war. My soul revolted against it; my heart revolted against it; but most of all my mind revolted against it. War, it seemed to me, was just a convention, as stupid and as evil as had been the convention of duelling. There may still be an individual

29

here and there who thinks that if one man accidentally
treads on another man's toe, he should rightly be called
upon to defend his life by taking the other man's life; but
most of us have outgrown such beliefs. Yet while such conventions existed, it seemed natural enough; just as it seems
natural now for a man to take his hat off when he meets a
woman whom he knows. But taking one's hat off is convention, not nature: as conventional as, and no more natural
than, raising the arm and saying *"Heil,* Hitler." War, I
felt, was not the human nature it was so often said to be,
but only a convention. When two individuals disagree,
they go, conventionally, to Law. When two nations dis-
agreed, and neither would give way, they went, equally
conventionally, to War. I did not see why the convention
should not be changed, so that they too went to Law.

Art may be summed up as integrity of aim. The art of
writing a play is to choose a theme and stick to it; the art of
fighting a war is to choose an objective and gain it. And the
art of writing *An Enquiry into the War Convention* is to
enquire into the conventions of war. Many readers told me
that I had ignored the economic causes of war. Of course
I had; just as in an earlier age I should have ignored the
sartorial causes of duels, however many had been fought
over the colour of a cravat. Had mankind decided to
eliminate all causes of duels, it would have had the impossible task of eliminating all differences of opinion. Mankind found it easier to eliminate, not the causes, but the
conventional result of such causes.

It is true that, if an economic or other cause of war can
be removed, there is so much less chance of war. If jealousy,
or other cause of murder, can be removed, there is so much
less opportunity for capital punishment. But capital punishment is not abolished in Chipping Norton just because

no murders are being committed there; nor is the war convention destroyed just because certain causes of war have been removed. A Greek cynic, ruminating on the cause of the Trojan war, would have said that it was silly to fight for ten years about a girl. But a Greek Pacifist, feeling strongly on the subject, would wish to do something more immediate than wait until man had become hermaphrodite and there were no girls to fight about. He would wish to destroy the convention that, if your wife got tired of you and left you for another man, "honour" demanded that for ten years your brother should kill everybody in sight, in order to advertise your extreme unattractiveness as a husband.

I was a Pacifist. I wished to destroy the conventional belief that war was an honourable way of settling international disputes. I wished to destroy the conventional definitions of "national honour" and "national prestige": the conventional acceptance of war by the Churches; the conventional glorification of war by the poets; I wished to destroy all that had been conventionally thought about war by those who had not thought about war; I wished my readers to look at modern war with their own eyes, not at a tradition of war through the eyes of their ancestors. That was why I called my book *An Enquiry into the War Convention*.

Strange Company

Writers are known, less by what they write, than by the labels which other people write for them: a misleading form of knowledge. I was now labelled "Pacifist". It was not long before I found myself invited into strange company. I was told that war would persist until capitalism was abolished, and I was invited to wear a red tie and join the Communist party. I was told that war would persist until the banks were abolished, and I was invited to wear a green shirt and support the Douglas Credit Scheme. I was told that war would persist until sin had been abolished, and I was invited to wear ashes on my head and be one with the Oxford Group. All these correspondents gave me the impression that what they really wanted was to establish their particular Utopia, leaving Peace to emerge, if she could, as one of the by-products. I accepted none of their invitations.

A year later I was privileged to meet Pacifists with no other axe to grind, but Pacifists with whom also (so much the worse for me, perhaps) I did not identify myself. It was a meeting, under the leadership of Dick Sheppard, of people not otherwise unknown, and now known to be ardent for Peace. For the most part, or so it seemed to me, they were concerned with their own personal conduct in the next war. They would not fight, of course; but could they conscientiously engage in non-combatant work? How would their souls feel if they succoured the wounded? Was that a betrayal of their principles? One speaker told us at great length of his experiences in the last war as a "total" conscientious objector. He had been imprisoned by the military on several occasions and as often had escaped. He had a technique, not only of escape but of passive resistance, warranted to baffle any ordinary sergeant-major, the secret of which he was prepared to pass on to all of us. It was clear that he had had a perfectly grand war; so much more interesting than mine. He was getting ready for another grand war.

Now in as far as I had a conscientious objection to war (and I doubt if "conscience" really came into it, for my

objection was more of the mind and the heart), I had a conscientious objection to war as an institution, not to the
faint possibility that in a particular war a rifle in my hands
might hit something. War seemed to me a wicked waste of
Life, of Time, of Beauty, of Opportunity, and I didn't
mind who stopped it, as long as it was stopped; I didn't
mind how it was stopped, as long as it was stopped. If it
could be stopped peacefully and quickly, so much the better; if it could only be stopped laboriously and at some loss
of life, so much the worse. The point was that this waste of
everything lovely in the world should not go on. Had it
been revealed to me by an angel in the night that Universal
and Perpetual Peace could only come, and would only
come, as the result of one more devastating war, I should
have said, "Good, let's start to-morrow. Whom do we fight?"
And my services, combatant or non-combatant as required,
would have been at the disposal of the Cause.

But, in any case, war had never seemed to me to be a
matter which concerned my personal conscience. It was a
matter which concerned the conscience of Civilisation. I
shared her guilt, and worked for her redemption. If there
were another war, then I had taken part in another war.
If there were Universal Peace, then, and only then, I had
renounced war for ever.

There was another respect in which I seemed to differ
from my fellow-pacifists. These were all talking as if their
real activities began when war was declared; but I knew
that when war was declared our activities ended; for we
had failed. I knew that it was impossible to preach the renunciation of war in war-time; for one would seem only to
be preaching the stopping of that particular war, and
preaching to only one of the combatants. By saying "*Stop
it, Bingo! Naughty* dog!" to a bull-terrier in a mix-up, one

does not advance the campaign for the muzzling of all loose dogs. I knew that the renunciation of war could only be effectively preached between wars; just as (I suppose, but I have never gone into the matter) the cause of Temperance can only be effectively preached between drinks.

Conscientious Objection

I think, perhaps, that that word "effectively" is the key to the sort of Pacifist I was, and am. In my young days a well-known Nonconformist preacher felt a conscientious objection to the payment of rates which provided religious education in schools. He did not (naturally) object to religious education in schools, but he objected to the particular form which it took. Having worked out the proportion of his payment devoted to education, and then the proportion of this proportion which might be supposed to sustain the little daily dose of religion, he deducted as it might be 15s. 6d. from his rates, and announced his readiness to die, or go to prison, on this point of conscience; the result being that the authorities distrained on his silver tea-pot. An admirer of the tenacity and religious fervour thus displayed would then buy him back the tea-pot for 15s. 6d., feeling that no man so good should be so wantonly deprived, and in another six months it would be all ready for the next distraint process. In this way a conscience was saved from sin, a Cause was advanced, and a tea-pot was kept in circulation.

Well, it may be that the Cause *was* advanced, for the ridiculousness of the proceedings provided some advertisement in the cheaper press; but only so, I felt, could this form of passive resistance be justified. To me passive resistance, civil disobedience, and conscientious objection were just ways of supporting a Cause in which one believed. If they failed, I was as ready to give it the conscientious support of civil obedience, or of active resistance to all its enemies. All I demanded was that the support should be effective.

I may be asked now if my "conscience" (and the tone of voice will certainly put it into inverted commas) will allow me to do *anything*, however wrong in itself, for a Cause in which I believe. Would it allow me, for instance, to lie? My only possible answer would be that it would depend on the Cause. But, broadly speaking, I may say that I consider my soul my own, as I consider my mind my own and my body my own. I should feel justified, though I might not have the courage, to risk my life, my body, to save another's.

I feel that I am equally justified in risking my soul to save the soul of another. My soul, my conscience, seem to me of small importance in comparison with the souls of millions. To prevent the corruption of the souls of all the children of the world, there is no sin which I would not commit. And in case this sounds heroic, I hurry to add that, in these circumstances, of course, it would not seem to me to be a sin.

This would appear to be the moment for some reference to a chapter in *Peace with Honour,* much applauded at the time by many, much condemned by others, and now continually quoted back at me; a chapter called "Onward Christian Soldiers". Well, I shall refer to it in its place. But I may say now that I am not seriously concerned to apologise for it, justify it, or (in the manner of many recent correspondents) get excited about it. "What did Mr. Gladstone say in 1874?" was once supposed to be the unanswerable question which would put any political candidate out of gear. "What did you say in 1934?" leaves me unmoved;

or would, if I were not afraid that the difference between 1934 and 1940 is less apparent to those who ask the question than it is to me. For there is a difference; and the difference can be given in one word. A Cabinet Minister, perhaps better informed than I, perhaps, though I hate to think it, more intelligent, said to me at the end of 1934: "I agreed with every word of your book—except one."

The word was *"Hitler"*.

II

Europe Was at Peace

Peace with Honour was begun in 1933. Hitler was Chancellor, but not yet in full power, nor fully self-exposed. Mussolini was in full power and, as always, in full voice, but as yet threatening nobody. On the surface Europe was at peace. Yet there they were: Hitler and Mussolini: men utterly without scruple. One could neither ignore them, nor appeal to their reason. One could only explain them away. I imagined a reader saying: "What is the good of talking about peace, and the abolition of armaments, and morality, and common sense: what is the good of reasoning at all? Abolish Germany, and there might be some hope of abolishing war." So for the space of a chapter called "Fascist Interlude", I tried to "abolish Germany": that is, to abolish the Hitler bogey.

My argument, briefly, was this: that though Fascism could only exist on the threat of war, it could not survive war; that is, that the aftermath of war in a Fascist country (or, likely enough, in any country) would be revolution, the nightmare of autocracy. The policy, therefore, of the Fascist autocrat was to threaten war rather than to make it:

to keep his people in subjection to his will by representing that their subjection was a military necessity for the safety or advancement of the state.

It was a good theory; it was true as far as it went. But it forgot that autocrats are not their own masters. Events are too much for them.

One Word—Hitler

If anybody reads *Peace with Honour* now, he must read it with that one word "HITLER" scrawled across every page. Before every irresistible conclusion to which I seek to draw him he must insert another premise: HITLER. Lord Randolph Churchill said on a famous occasion that he "forgot Goschen". I "forgot Hitler"—Hitler as we now know him. Perhaps I should have known then; perhaps I could not have known. Though the book was written in such ignorance, perhaps it was worth writing; for that disfiguring word "Hitler" does not blot out every line, nor cancel all the truths. Perhaps on balance it would have been better unwritten. All this would be grotesquely unimportant if I were merely trying to defend myself. But if I say, as I would wish to say, "Never mind what I said in 1934, listen to me *now*", I cannot escape the retort: "If you were right then, why need we? If you were wrong then, why should we?" And since I want to be listened to now, I must make this attempt to keep the ear of the Pacifists who listened to me once, in order that I may explain to them, not why one ardent Pacifist has suddenly become, as they would say, a "violent militarist", but why it is the very ardour of his Pacifism, unchanged since 1934, which inspires his passion now for military victory.

"Onward Christian Soldiers"

Every one of us has had the experience of writing a letter which is totally misunderstood by the reader. Why? We have used simple words, words of only one meaning, and have expressed ourselves clearly and in reasonably good English. We thought we were writing a friendly letter, and are shocked to find that it has been bitterly resented. Why has this happened? Simply because the spirit behind the letter as we wrote, the background of the letter, was left out of the envelope. A quotation, a family joke, will have a false meaning for one who does not see the unwritten inverted commas; an innocent anecdote may seem to refer to something of which, in fact, the writer had no knowledge. Words can say much and leave much unsaid.

I turned just now to a page in that chapter of which I was talking, "Onward Christian Soldiers", and read the realistic description of war to which the following words are the postscript: "This is war. No Church condemns it. Bishops approve heartily of it. Accredited Chaplains accompany the combatants to see that the religious side of their life is not neglected. What does it all mean? Does one laugh or does one cry?"

The description of war begins thus:

"Two nations are in dispute about something. . . . It seems to be, and may in fact be, to the material advantage of either to enforce possession of it!"

It ends thus:

"When the fortitude of one government gives way, the government of the winning nation settles the original cause of dispute by taking as much of the loser's wealth or territory as it can profitably assimilate."

A little later, in an imaginary cross-examination of a clergyman, he is made to say:

C. "Do you really mean that you are prepared for a German army to march through the streets of London, for Germany to dictate whatever humiliating terms she pleases, to exact indemnities, to make unlawful annexations, to——?"

M. "I am not prepared for, in the sense of being happily acquiescent in, any of these things. In fact I should hate them. It would be easy to feel intensely humiliated by them. . . . But we don't go killing people in order to relieve or prevent our humiliation. Whence do you get this extraordinary idea that, though man must suffer all things rather than do wrong, a nation can do all the wrong it likes rather than suffer anything. . . ?"

And a little later:

M. "You see what I'm looking for, don't you? The point where Christianity ends and Patriotism begins."

War as We Knew It

Now why does the one unwritten word "Hitler" make it plain to any intelligent person that I was not writing, and could not have been writing, with a foreknowledge of 1935–39? Well, let us look at some of the words which I did write.

In the first passage: *Material advantage.*

In the second passage: *Wealth.*

In the third passage: *Indemnities . . . humiliation.*

In the fourth passage: *Patriotism.*

Read the book again, read any passage again, and you see

at once that it is a pre-Hitler book. It is an indictment of war as we knew it; war to which both sides were a party because both sides agreed to the convention; the convention that "patriotism" rightly preferred war to "humiliation" or "insult": that war was justified by economic causes or the need for living-room: that "prestige" was something worth killing for; the convention that if some small material advantage was withheld from a country by another, "honour" demanded that she should suffer (among other things) the infinitely greater material disadvantage of a war, on the fifty-fifty chance that she would get the smaller advantage which she had once needed.

Now that is the "background" of the book: my detestation of the wickedness of war as a killing for material ends, of the stupidity of war as a conventional sacrifice out of all proportion to the material ends gained. This intense feeling in my mind inspired the book; led me to write it with the fervour of the crusader rather than with the detachment of the scientist. I withdraw none of it as an indictment of war in 1934; I offer none of it as an indictment against our share of the war of 1939.

Hitler has made just that difference.

Total Conquest

For Hitler does not only make total war, he makes, or seeks to make, total conquest; conquest, not only of the material possessions of a country, but of its bodies and souls. When Hitler conquers, the Gestapo rules. Describe what is happening to Poland now in the most moderate language which your feelings will allow you, and you will not find yourself using such words as "humiliation", "insult" and "material loss". Hitler's "war" is not the international war we know. It is a war for the destruction of all Christian and civilised values. Not a war between nations, but a war between Good and Evil. Hitler is a crusader against God; just that.

There is no argument about this. It is all set out by himself in Rauschning's book, *Hitler Speaks*. In Hitler's view the ordinary man has no right to an independent spiritual existence; he is intended for use in a machine; and when he is in Hitler's power, he will be so used. Hitler is literally the enemy of Humanity, for he does not believe in Humanity. He is the self-elected, self-confessed anti-Christ. Evil is his good.

Well, do we resist him?

The Pacifist Argues

I have heard two arguments used by those who, believing that he is this, still hesitate to resist him. The first takes this form:

"You say that he seeks to conquer our souls. He cannot. Man's soul is unconquerable. An enemy may take our possessions from us, he may harm our bodies, but he cannot force us into doing wrong. He cannot corrupt our souls. God has told us to suffer all things for His sake; our very sufferings will be a testimony to Him."

We need waste no time in a theological argument on the ethics of martyrdom. The answer is simply this. Man's soul may be unconquerable, but a child's soul is not. Hitler *can* corrupt the souls of children; he *has* corrupted the souls of hundreds of thousands of children. He has deliberately trained the Hitler Youth to cruelty. He has "hardened" them against all danger of spiritual infection. He has dehumanised them, and used them.

Do we resist him?

The other argument is—well, it is not so much an argument as a woolly-minded hangover from some earlier war. It takes the form of saying that Hitler may be Evil, but are we Good? Look at our own record! Who are *we* to talk? And so on.

Well, who is anybody to talk at any time? Because one is fighting against Evil, and consequently for Good against Evil, one does not claim to be entirely good. One can rescue a cat from a boy who is ill-treating it, whether or not one has borrowed thirty shillings from the cashbox to put on the 2.30. Even if in the past we had committed the very evil which we are now fighting (and we have not), we could, and should, fight it now.

But I should like to say something about this matter of "our own record". One of those who wrote to me about *Peace with Honour* was a German from Hamburg. Whether his letter was written freely or as a piece of organised propaganda I do not know. But he expressed agreement with such of the book as did not criticise Nazi Germany, and assured me of the peaceful happiness of all Germans under Nazi rule. In reply I said that I couldn't help feeling doubtful of the happiness of some of the Germans in concentration camps. He made the obvious German retort: "Look at your own record! What about the concentration camps in South Africa?"

Well, that was easy. I didn't defend, nor want to defend, the concentration camps in South Africa. I didn't bother to point out that the identity between the two "concentrations" was an identity of name only. All that needed to be said was this: In England, thousands of people could, did, and were freely allowed to, condemn the concentration camps; in Germany anybody who opened his mouth about them was sent to one himself. That is the difference between Liberty and Tyranny, between Good and Evil. We are not, after all, such unworthy representatives of the Good.

German Peace

As Pacifists have so often pointed out, when one has accepted nine wars, it is easy to accept the tenth without thinking. But it is just as easy, when one has condemned nine wars, to condemn the tenth without thinking. The Militarist says "War is human nature", and with these words abandons thought. It would be a pity if the Pacifist were to abandon thought when once he had said "War is wicked".

For he would be making just the mistake which he has so often condemned in the militarist: that of loyalty to a word whose meaning has changed.

In 1934 I wrote "The word War has lost its meaning. It is no longer War. It is something for which the word has not yet been invented, something as far removed from the Napoleonic Wars as they were from a boxing match." I begged my readers, therefore, to forget all which they had ever thought about War, and to think all over again about Modern War. For "as a *new* thought Modern War is completely unthinkable."

The word Peace has now lost its meaning. It is no longer Peace. I beg my readers to forget all which they have ever thought about Peace, and to think all over again about German Peace: the Peace which Poland (no longer at war) is now experiencing. For as a *new* thought German Peace is completely unthinkable.

In 1934 I wrote "Modern War means, quite definitely, and without any mental escape, choking and poisoning and torturing to death thousands of women and children. Whether you are Christian or Jew, atheist or agnostic, you have got to fit acceptance of this into your philosophy of life. . . . Here is the fact now and you have got to justify to yourself your acceptance of it; and the justification has got to be based on such ultimate truths as will always be sacred to you."

That was addressed to the Church in 1934: "Onward Christian Soldiers". I address it to myself now. I accept the facts, and I accept this war. For German Peace means all that Modern War means—and worse. It means not only the torturing to death of bodies but the poisoning to death of souls. . . . And the ultimate truth which will always be sacred is that the soul is more important than the body.

To-day we cannot choose between the Heaven of Peace and the Hell of War. We must choose between two Hells. The Hell of "Peace" which we have rejected lies at the very bottom of the abyss.

Crying "Wolf"

The fable of the boy who amused himself by crying "Wolf!" so often that the villagers no longer believed him when the wolf came is used, like all fables, to point a moral. The moral is directed against the boy. "Silly boy! See what happened to him!" But the moral might equally be directed against the villagers. Silly villagers! See what happened to *them!* For, though the boy may have been no great loss, they also lost their flocks. Did they deserve to lose them? Let us consider the reasoning which went on in a villager's mind.

1. This boy said "Wolf!" three times when there was no wolf.
2. It is therefore certain that there is no wolf this time.

Could any reasoning be sillier? What he should have thought was:

1. The boy is only there because it is extremely likely that a wolf *will* come one day.
2. It is certain that, when the wolf does come, the boy will call out.
3. It is not certain, after the thrashing I gave him yesterday, that he will call out again if the wolf doesn't come.
4. Therefore the chances are that the wolf *is* here.

And even if it turned out to be another false alarm, the reasoning would be just as true at the next alarm. Stupid, stupid villagers!

To many Pacifists (indeed, to all who write to me) the great stumbling-block in the way is the fact that "Wolf!" has been cried before.

"A war to end war?" they say derisively. "You said that of the last war!"

"Hitler is the devil?" they jeer. "You said that of the Kaiser!"

"This war is different from any other war? Why, you yourself pointed out that militarists said that of every war!"

"We are fighting for Freedom? How you derided these fights for Freedom!"

"We are fighting for God? How fiercely you attacked the Churches for identifying God with their country!"

It is a very good retort; it would carry the house in any school debating society; but it doesn't *prove* that there is no wolf.

I wrote somewhere once that the third-rate mind was only happy when it was thinking with the majority, the second-rate mind was only happy when it was thinking with the minority, and the first-rate mind was only happy when it was thinking. With equal truth it may be said that a first-rate mind is not one which does not remember the past, nor is it one which cannot forget the past; it is a mind which will use the past but not be ordered by it. It is a mind independent of everybody and everything but the facts in front of it. It is as little perturbed to find itself sharing a thought with the simple as it is elated to find itself sharing a thought with the subtle. It will fight for what it has discovered to be right, as happily in the serried ranks of the Blimps as in the lonely company of the Shaws.

Even though all the stupid militarists cried "Wolf!" when there was no wolf, yet the wolf is at our door now. Even though all the clever Pacifists said that there was no wolf, when there was no wolf, yet the wolf is at our door now. If we cling to the theory that wolves are delightful creatures when treated kindly as cubs, then perhaps this one wasn't treated kindly as a cub. If we proved conclusively six years ago that wolves never came as far west as England, then perhaps this one has escaped from a zoo, or is some foul hybrid unknown to zoology. What does it matter how right or wrong we were in the past? There is death, and worse than death, waiting for ourselves and our children. What do we do?

III

Three Possibilities

In theory there are three possibilities:

1. The victory of Britain.
2. The victory of Germany.
3. Peace without victory:
   (*a*) leaving Germany in possession of what she has already won;
   (*b*) leaving Germany in possession of no more of German Europe than is agreed to be rightfully hers.

This last possibility (3), in either alternative, is "PEACE NOW!", the slogan of certain Pacifists.

Now I have said that I was the sort of Pacifist who was concerned to make his pacifism effective. I don't mean by this that I refuse to write anything about Peace unless everybody promises to read it; nor that, when they have read it, I expect them immediately to act on it. I mean that I put down what I think in the most effective words I know, and I take care that the book so written is put before the public in the most effective way. If, as a result, I persuade ten people to accept the Cause, then I have made an effective contribution to the Cause. If, by reason of bad writing, illogical argument, or ill-timed publication, I persuade nobody, then, even though my own passionate love of Peace shines out as clearly, I consider myself by this much the less a Pacifist, that I have brought nothing to the Cause but my own ineffective self.

I am still a Pacifist, but I hope a practical Pacifist. I still want to abolish war. Which of these three possibilities gives us the best chance of abolishing war? None gives us a certainty; but which gives us the most effective taking-off place?

Victory for Germany means that Britain, like the rest of Europe, comes under German Peace. I have already said that in my own opinion such Peace is worse than War. Were I alive to see it, as I hope I shall not be, I should want to write an indictment of "Peace". Other Pacifists might still feel that War was the great enemy. Would they be in a good position to indict it? Not from the concentration camps where, under German rule, all good Pacifists go. They know, and I know, that we should only be able to write or to preach what Goebbels, or some contemptible Fascist representative of his, instructed us to write, or allowed us to preach.

Peace without Victory, or *"Peace Now"*. In considering this, the practical Pacifist has two questions to ask himself: "Can I help to bring it about?" "When it comes, can I make effective use of it?"

If he thinks that a victory for Britain will best advance the Cause, he *can* help to bring victory to Britain.

If he thinks that a victory for Germany will best advance the Cause, he *can* help to bring victory to Germany.

But can he help to stop the war *now?*

No. He may talk, he may write, he may distribute pamphlets, he may shout himself hoarse on soap-boxes, but he is not stopping the war. If Hitler and Göring were listening, and nodding their heads, and saying "This man Hopkinson talks extraordinary good sense——" But no, that is not fair. It would be enough if they could hear him; so that he could say: "Well, I did my best. I told them, and if they didn't believe me, it is not my fault." But he knows that they can't hear him; he knows that nothing which he preaches has the slightest effect on Germany. Yet, even so, he might say: "It is for me to preach to *my* countrymen, it is for like-minded Germans to preach to *theirs*. Between us we shall stop the war." Yes, that would be an answer . . . did he not know that like-minded Germans are shot or put in concentration camps when they preach.

So then, only one of the combatants, England, is being told to stop the war. If England could stop the war, "leaving Germany in possession of no more of German Europe than is agreed to be rightfully hers", then England would have won the war. If England did stop the war, "leaving Germany in possession of what she had already won", then England would have lost the war. So that when the Pacifist bellows "Stop the war!" he is either bellowing "Win the war!" which is what we are trying to do, or "Surrender!" which is what Germany is trying to make us do. In neither case is he helping to bring about Peace without Victory.

"Peace without Victory"

The Pacifist's cry "Stop the War!" is, then, wholly ineffective in bringing about the desired result. Peace without Victory. But even if it were effective, would Peace without Victory be an effective taking-off place for the abolition of war?

One has often heard the argument: The only hope for a stable world after the war is an agreed Peace now, for Peace *with* Victory creates nothing but bitterness and the seeds of future wars. Now if this were true: if, that is, the fact that it has been true in the past made it a truth for all time: then the Cause is lost. For Germany has already won "Peace with Victory" over Austria, Czechoslovakia, Poland, Denmark, Norway, Holland, Belgium, Luxemburg and France. Bitterness and the seeds of future wars have been sown so lavishly over the greater part of Europe, that there is no hope for a stable world. It may be answered that, if we came to an agreed peace with Germany now, we could "doubtless" (which means that the speaker would rather not explain how) arrange with Germany that these countries should be restored. Excellent. But this means that Germany can conquer *nine* countries, remain herself unconquered, and yet sow no seeds of future wars. If the Pacifist believes this, why is he so afraid of Britain conquering *one* country?

The truth is, of course, that, as between the nations of Europe, Peace without Victory is now impossible. The victories have been obtained. As between England and Germany it is still possible. And then what?

Peace without Victory means that Hitler is still in power. Now two facts stand out so obviously that it is almost ridiculous to call attention to them: as if one stood at the top of Ludgate Hill with a friend and said: "I don't know if you've noticed any sort of church in the neighbourhood."

1. We cannot dethrone Hitler (and Mussolini) except by defeating them.
2. Until Hitler and Mussolini are dethroned, proposals for the abolition of war must be completely ineffective.

Here are Mussolini's own words:

"Fascism does not believe either in the possibility or in the utility of perpetual peace. A doctrine that is based on the premise of peace is foreign to Fascism."

We need not bother to look for similar words from Hitler. Action speaks louder. We know what happened to the German winner of the Nobel Peace Prize. . . .

It seems, then, that the Pacifist can neither help to obtain, nor make any effective use of, Peace without Victory.

This leaves, as the only possibility offering him any hope for the Cause, *Victory for Britain*.

For Democracy

Victory for Britain is a victory for democracy over autocracy. There is no hope for the Cause except through democracy.

There are two reasons for thinking this. The first is that we have reached a stage in human progress when the vast majority of the peoples of the world are Pacifists. This is due partly to the bitter lessons we have learnt as to the complete futility of war; partly to our knowledge of the increasing barbarity of war; and mostly to our realisation that the horrors of war must now be endured, not only by professional warriors, but by every one of us.

But though the peoples of the world are Pacifists, individuals in the world are not. The march of civilization is like the march of a medieval army. There are skirmishers in front, there is a main body, there are stragglers. In estimating the advance of civilization no account is taken of the stragglers. If we say that we are cleaner than our forefathers, we are not thinking of tramps and verminous children. If we say that we are less credulous, we are not thinking of the fools who run and the fools who read the Sunday astrologer's column. And so, if we say, and say rightly, that we are now more humane, more alive to and shocked by the evils of the Rule of Force, we are leaving out of our reckoning the individual gangster and the individual murderer. In a democratic country the people, the main body of troops, mark the stage of civilization which that country has reached: a stage of civilization which is now beyond war. But in a totalitarian state the gangster may easily be the autocrat. This is one reason why the people (democracy) offer a safeguard for peace which cannot be offered by the individual (autocracy).

The other reason is this: a totalitarian state by definition exists for the benefit of the state, not for the benefit of its members. But if the state claims to have a life of its own to which the life of every individual is subordinate, then its life can only be a life in competition with other states; its only victories victories over its competitors. One can see that this must be so if one imagines a group of islanders in the Pacific, cut off from the rest of mankind, forming themselves into a totalitarian state, in which each individual is told, "Nothing which happens to *you* matters; the only thing which matters is the welfare of the island." We see that this is nonsense; we see that the only "welfare of the island" conceivable is the welfare of each individual islander. And we see that a totalitarian island can only justify its existence by competing with, and obtaining victories over, neighbouring islands. Inevitably a successful war is the complete victory, the ultimate form of the island-state's self-expression.

It is clear, therefore, that whether Hitlerism, Mussoliniism, Stalinism and any similar form of government are to be regarded as the expression of a genuine political doctrine or merely as an excuse for autocracy, they are, they must be, a barrier to the peace of the world. If this war ensures the triumph of democracy, and only if so, then it may end war.

Yes, I know that we said the last war would end war—and it didn't. And the Wright Brothers said of each successive immature aeroplane that it would fly—and it didn't. And each successive expedition said that it would get to the Pole—and it didn't. But men did not give up hope, and in the end they won. Are we Pacifists really such cowards that we, alone among men, surrender the Cause at the first failure? I cannot believe it.

"I Believe . . ."

When one argues about something which seems self-evident, when one tries to prove something for which no proof seems needed, it is difficult to know where to begin, and when to stop. If I were trying to prove to a friend that two sixpences were of the same value as a shilling I might find myself saying, "Well, you admit, I suppose, that twice six is twelve?" If the answer were a dogged "No", I should hold my head in my hands, and think: "Now is it any good asking if he admits that twice one is two? Dare I risk it? Because if he doesn't, where am I? How much farther back can we go?"

Possibly my friend, who is convinced that two sixpences make half a crown, is subject to the same misgivings.

Well, I believe that twice one is two, and I also believe these things:

I believe that Nazi rule is the foulest abomination with which mankind has ever been faced.

I believe that, if it is unresisted, it will spread over, and corrupt, the whole world.

I believe that no decent man, no humane man, no honest man; no man of courage, intelligence or imagination; no man who ever had a kindly thought for his neighbour or compassion for the innocent; no lover of truth, no lover of beauty, no lover of God could have a place in that world.

I believe, therefore, that it is as much the duty of mankind to reject such a world as it is the duty of any community to reject gangster rule.

I see no way of doing this save by the use of force.

I am not frightened by words. If this use of force be called International War, then for the first time in my life I approve of International War; if it be called Civil War, then, not for the first time, I approve of Civil War. If it be compared with the action of policemen, then, as often before, I am in favour of action by policemen. If it be called Resistance to Evil, then, as (I hope) always, I am for resistance to evil.

Only when we have resisted it and overcome it can Civilization resume its march.

To America

Perhaps I can best come to an end by quoting from some lines which I addressed to America at the beginning of May:

Yes, "War is Hell."
And Peace is Hell, if it's Peace with the Devil in power.
Yet, if this is not your quarrel, and not your hour,
If you have chosen Peace, you have chosen well.
But—scatter your armies, burn your ships,
Tear the breech-block out of the gun;
Never again can you fight who fight not now,
No rallying-call can ever rise to your lips,
There lives no faith to which you can make your vow,
There is no Cause to fight for; only the one,
Only one gage of battle, only one battle-song:
Right against Wrong.

NORDIC TWILIGHT

By

E. M. FORSTER

A speech of Antigone, a single sentence of Socrates, a few lines that were inscribed on an Indian rock before the Second Punic War, the footsteps of a silent yet prophetic people who dwelt by the Dead Sea and perished in the fall of Jerusalem, come nearer to our lives than the ancestral wisdom of barbarians who fed their swine on the Hercynian acorns.

ACTON, *The Study of History*

Vain de se lamenter (et un peu dégoûtant). Vain aussi, et dangereux, de trop séparer les hauts dirigeants et le peuple allemand. Ils semblent avoir réalisé ce que je déteste calmement mais le plus au monde: une pyramide d'appétits à base de stupidité.

Letter from a French writer, September 1939

NORDIC TWILIGHT

THIS pamphlet is propaganda. I believe that if the Nazis won they would destroy our civilisation. I want to say why I think this. I want to persuade others to think as I do.

What Use Is Culture?

Civilisation, culture, art, literature, music, philosophy—it is difficult to discourse on such topics without sounding unreal. As soon as one tries to defend them, they seem to matter less, or to matter only to a small and sheltered clique. In wartime especially do they lose prestige; why worry about civilisation when people are in pain? It is unconvincing to look solemn and say, through half-closed lips: "I do worry, I must worry." "All right, worry away, you're lucky to have the time to do it in," is the natural retort. Thousands of people since last September have gone bored and cynical over culture; they will fight for their homes and their friends, for their country, for the Empire, for the present economic system, for a new economic system, they will fight because they see nothing else to do—but as far as they are concerned the Nazis can burn all our books and forbid us to write any new ones. What odds will it make if culture closes down in these islands? A few professors and poets will go on the dole, but who cares? This cynicism is not confined to toughs; it has spread to the B.B.C., from whose programmes English literature is now almost entirely excluded, and it has been voiced by a Cabinet Minister.

I believe such cynicism to be unsound, for the reason that it ignores the strange nature of man. Man needs the intangible. He cannot live by bread alone. He has developed away from the other animals because the non-material fascinated him, because he wanted to understand things which are useless (philosophy), or to make things which are useless (literature and art). Philosophy, literature and art may have begun in magic, and magic may have seemed useful once, but the curious creature continued to pursue them after they had been discredited. He needed the life of the spirit. This may have been a blunder on Man's part, but he has made it irrevocably, and to-day if you give him bread only, he becomes unwell. The intangible has become a stimulant necessary for his physical health. For a proof of this, glance at any close-up photograph of German soldiers and airmen. Observe the expression on their faces. Something is amiss. They are hefty, they may be heroic, they may even look intelligent besides, but they are blank. It is desolating to see such blankness in the eyes of young people even when they are our most dangerous enemies, who would destroy us without mercy if they landed here. It means that they have been cheated of their inheritance by a perverted education, they have been ruined mentally so that they may better spread ruin. The Nazis want all people to have that same terrifying empty look. They hate the life of the spirit and all the disinterested activities which prove that the spirit is at work and enjoying itself. They would not admit this, and some of their culture-theories are most elevating on paper and constantly refer to the soul. Viewing them from outside

Germany, we know better, and if we in England start belittling literature and art as some of our leaders are doing, and sneering at the intangible, we shall really be playing their game.

They are doomed to oppose anything that challenges party-loyalty. It is their fate, they cannot now escape it, and books, pictures, even music, have become, like religion, their foe. They imprison a particular writer, blow up a particular monument, ban a particular tune, slash a particular canvas, but the menace survives. They say to their people: "Don't worry, and don't dare to worry; the soul of man, like his body, belongs to the State, and we will tell you what to read and when to read, and when to stop reading, when to applaud and when to hiss." Their people obey, but outside their borders there is disobedience and they are obliged to make war. They will fail—not through any military miscalculation, but because they misconceive the nature of man. Man will resist totalitarianism through his inability to live on bread alone. The fight will be hard, because never before has the State been so strong, or studied so carefully how to influence the herd. But Man's deep-rooted individual psychology, his innate longing for freedom, will save him. He cannot be driven back into the forest now. He has, to preserve his sanity, the example of his own past. Of the peoples whom Germany tramples to-day, perhaps the Czechs suffer most. Yet it is a Czech poet who writes:—

> Truth has not lost its power;
> Reading old prophecies, we believe in Resurrection.[1]

[1] Jiri Zhor, *Sursum Corda*.

What Use Is Freedom?

This desire for freedom is bound up with the whole culture-question. The Nazis condemn freedom, in practice and theory, and assert that culture will flourish without it. Individualists like myself believe in its desirability, and for three reasons.

The first reason concerns the writer (the artist generally, the writer more particularly). He must *feel* free. If he doesn't he may find it difficult to fall into the creative mood. He must have the sense of owning infinite treasures, even if he does not choose to use them, he must rule the past, present and future like a king, however moderate his actual equipment. If he *feels* free, sure of himself, unafraid, easy inside, he is in a favourable condition for the act of creation, and may do good work.

The second reason also concerns the writer. To *feel* free is not enough. It may be enough for the mystic, who can function alone and can shut himself up and concentrate even in a concentration camp. The writer, the artist, needs something more: freedom to tell other people what he is feeling. "La liberté de penser est la liberté de communiquer sa pensée," says Salvador de Madariaga, which epigram hits off the situation neatly. Madariaga then points out that one individual can only communicate with another by physical means, by a bridge of matter, and that the power controlling the bridge controls the messages passing over the bridge, and may stop them from getting across. This, of course, is what the Nazis are doing. They do not, they cannot, prevent freedom to think or feel, though they would no doubt condemn it from the National-Socialist point of view, as a selfish waste of time. They do, and can, prevent freedom to communicate. The knowledge that they can do this reacts disastrously on the artist. He cannot function in a vacuum like the mystic, he cannot spin tales in his head, or paint pictures in the air, or hum tunes under his breath. He must have an audience, and knowing that he may be forbidden to express his feelings, he becomes afraid to feel. Officials, even when they are well-meaning, do not realise this. Their make-up is so different from the artist's. They assume that, when they censor a work, only the work in question is affected; they do not realise that they may have impaired the creative machinery of the mind.

The third reason for freedom concerns the general public. The public must be free to receive, to read, to listen, to look. If it is prevented from receiving the communications which the artist sends, it becomes, like him, inhibited, though in a different way; it remains immature, and gets the blank look of those unhappy German soldiers and airmen.

I do not want to exaggerate the claims of freedom. Freedom does not guarantee the production of masterpieces, and masterpieces have been produced under conditions far from free.[1] Freedom is only a favourable step—or rather three little steps. When artists feel easy, when they can express themselves openly, and when the public is allowed to receive their communications, there is a chance of good work being produced and of the general level of civilisation rising. Before the war, it was rising a little in England, it was rising in France, Czecho-Slovakia, Scandinavia, the Netherlands. In Germany it was falling. Her achievements in art and literature, in speculation, in pure science, were contemptible. But she was perfecting her instruments

[1] For example, the Aeneid and the plays of Racine.

of destruction, and she now hopes to reduce neighbouring cultures to the same level as her own by their aid.

Our Culture Is National

Our culture over here is national. It has not been imposed on us by a government department, but springs naturally out of our way of looking at things, and out of the way we have looked at things in the past. It has developed slowly, and easily, and one might say lazily; the English countryside, the English sense of humour, the English love of fair play, English prudishness and smugness, English freakishness, the mild English idealism and good-humoured reasonableness have all combined to produce something which is certainly not perfect, but which may claim to be unusual. Our great achievement has been in literature; here we stand in the first rank, both as regards prose and verse. We have not done much in painting and music, and zealots who pretend that we have only make us look silly. We have made a respectable and sensible contribution to philosophy. And—to revert for a moment to this question of freedom—we pay homage to freedom even when we have not got it and homage is better than abuse: it leaves the shrine open, and the god is more likely to return.

Now when a culture is genuinely national, as ours has been, it is capable, when the hour strikes, of becoming supernational [1] and contributing to the general good of humanity. It gives and takes. It wants to give and take. It has generosity and modesty, it is not confined by political and geographic boundaries, it does not fidget about purity

[1] I write "supernational" because "international" has now fallen into such bad company that it is restricted to conferences.

of race or mythical origins in a forest, it does not worry about survival, but living in the present and sustained by the desire to create, it expands wherever human beings are to be found. Our civilisation was ready to do this when the hour struck, and the civilisation of France was ahead of us, ready too. We did not want England to be England for ever, it seemed to us a meagre destiny. We hoped for a world to which, when it had been made one by science, England could contribute. Science has duly unified the world. The hour has struck. Neither England nor France can contribute. Why?

The historian of the future, and he alone, will be able to answer this question authoritatively. He will see, as we cannot, the true perspective of this crisis, and it may appear to him as small as the crisis of 1914 already appears to us. The so-called "great" war was obviously a little one, and our present troubles may be the prelude to a still vaster upheaval which we cannot expect to understand. We must answer out of our ignorance, and as well as we can. And to my limited outlook, Hitler's Germany is the villain, it is she who has prevented the other nations from contributing to the supernational, it is she who, when the hour struck, ruined the golden moment and ordered an age of bloodshed.

German Culture Is Governmental

Germany, like ourselves, has had a great national culture, but during this century she made the disastrous mistake of allowing that culture to become governmental. She was supreme in music, eminent in philosophy, weak (like ourselves) in the visual arts, gifted in literature. Incidentally (and I think this has been part of her malady) she had a deeper sense than ourselves of the Tragic in life. Seriously minded, she felt that there must lie ahead for herself or for someone an irreparable disaster. That was the mentality of Wagner, and perhaps the present war may be considered as a scene (we do not yet know which) out of the *Nibelung's Ring*. I listen to Wagner to-day with unchanged admiration and increasing anxiety. Here is a world in which someone must come to grief, and with the maximum of orchestration and scenery. The hero slays or is slain, Hunding kills Siegmund, Siegfried kills the dragon, Hagen Siegfried, Brunnhilde leaps into the flames and brings down the Halls of Earth and Heaven. The tragic view of the universe can be noble and elevating, but it is a dangerous guide to daily conduct, and it may harden into a stupid barbarism, which smashes at problems instead of disentangling them. It hopes to destroy; if it fails, it commits suicide, and it cannot see that God may be wanting it to do neither. Göring, perched up in a castle with his drinking cups and plunder, and clamouring for Fate, is a Wagnerian hero gone wrong, an anachronism which has abused the name and the true nature of Tragedy.

However, the basic trouble with German culture is not that it has developed the tragic view of life, but that it has become governmental. Having done that, it must cease to be national. It has lost its spontaneity, it can produce nothing which has not been approved at headquarters, and it can never become supernational and contribute to the general uplift of humanity. Germany is to be Germany for ever, and more German with each generation. "What is 'to be German'?" asks Hitler, and replies: "The best answer to this question does not define, it lays down a law." [1]

[1] Hitler: *Die Kunst ist in den Völkern begründet*. Munich, 1937.

Thus enfranchised, his country presses on to a goal which can be described in exalted language, but which is the goal of a fool. For all the time she shouts and tramples her neighbours, the clock of the world moves on, and science makes the world one. "Gangsterdom for ever" is a possibility, and the democracies are fighting against it. "Germany for ever" is an uneducated official's dream.

When a national culture becomes governmental it always has to be exploited, and falsified. For it never quite suits the bureaucratic book. The words and the images that have come down through the centuries are often contradictory; they represent a bewildering wealth of human experience which it is our privilege to enjoy, to examine and to build on. A free country allows its citizens this privilege. A totalitarian country daren't because it fears diversity of opinion. The heritage of the past has to be overhauled, so that the output of the present may be standardised, and the output of the present has to be standardised, or Germany would cease to be Germany. Nothing could be more logical than the dreary blind alley down which the Nazis advance, and down which they would like to herd the whole human family. It leads nowhere, not even into Germany. They have got into it because they have worshipped the State. They are determined to destroy the civilisation of England, and from their point of view most reasonably; they are already trying to destroy the civilisations of the Czechs and the Poles, and a few years ago, before Mussolini became Nordic, they denounced the Mediterranean, too, as dangerous, decadent and dark. It is tempting to call them "wicked" and be done, but wicked is not a word I find easy to use—not through any innate charity, but because it seldom fits the facts. I see Göring not as Hagen but as Kundry: under a curse. Wherever they encounter variety and spontaneity the Nazis are doomed to attack. Germany's very gifts, her own high cultural achievement, must be recompounded, and turned to poison, in order that the achievements of others may perish.

WHAT HAS GERMANY DONE TO THE GERMANS?

Germany had to make war on her own people before she could attack Europe. It was a war which lasted several years, and was conducted with incredible cruelty. Thousands and thousands of her citizens were robbed, tortured, interned, expelled, killed. When she had got rid of them, she was in a position to transfer operations, and start against France and England. To the eye of the historian, the whole will probably appear as a single process, in which the antithesis between "peace" and "war" seems old-fashioned. The 1914 war was not like this one; it was not preluded by floods of refugees, the Kaiser's Germany still formed part of the European fabric, she was still a country though a hostile one. To-day she is not a hostile country, she is a hostile theory; the Nazis by their own wish and by their own declaration, are a principle apart.

Let me recall a few of the incidents of Germany's war against Germans. I shall not be so much concerned with physical persecutions as with her attempts to bully and twist the mind.

The Nazis are not fools—it is a typical British mistake to keep making fun of them—and their teachings exhibit much nobility and common-sense; that the nobility is spurious and the common-sense perverted, does not immediately appear. For instance, they teach, and very plausibly, that instinct is superior to reason, and character more important than book-learning. Hitler says, "What we suffer from to-day is an excess of education." [1] Göring: "We want no National Socialists of the brain." [2] Goebbels: "The intellect is a danger to the shaping of the character." [3] Baldur von Schirach: "The Intellectual's progress went through the gate beneath the inscription 'Knowledge is Might' into a land of negation. . . . It is against these cold calculators that our movement rose. It is, and always has been, a revolution of the Soul. . . . It reveals that power which the Intellectual will deny, since it is as inconceivable to him as is the God who gave it: the power of the soul and sentiment." [4]

The List of Martyrs

This reads very well, but why does the soul always require a machine-gun? Why can the character only cope with the intellect when it has got it inside a concentration camp and is armed with a whip? Why does the instinct instinctively persecute? On the surface the Nazi creed is congenial, and it misled some simple-minded people in this country; scratch the surface, and you find intolerance and cruelty. The list of the martyrs is long, and will never be revealed until Judgment Day, but as regards German writers and artists of distinction there are scarcely any who have not suffered. I take at random the case of a sculptor, Benno Elkan, who is in England to-day, and whose work can be seen in Westminster Abbey and at Cambridge; Elkan had to leave Germany in 1933 because the Nazis

[1] *Danziger Vorposten*, 5.2.38.
[2] Speech, 9.4.33.
[3] *Michael*, a short story, Munich 1934.
[4] Speech, 15.1.38.

were systematically destroying his creations, in particular his public monuments, which included the memorial to Stresemann at Mainz. I take a friend of my own—a writer who escaped from Vienna, a charming fellow, whose crime it was to be a Jew. I take another friend, also a writer, a pure-blooded Aryan from Berlin, whose crime it was to think. I take the classical case of Thomas Mann—the greatest novelist in Germany, a man of international reputation, who wants to be left at peace, and to write; he is in exile.[1] Heinrich Mann, Arnold and Stefan Zweig, Leon Feuchtwanger, Emil Ludwig . . . the list extends . . . the musicians Adolf and Fritz Busch, Artur Schnabel, Paul Hindemith, Arnold Schönberg . . . they were not criminals, were not even politicians hostile to the regime. They were artists, but the regime insists that culture should be governmental, and worships force. "We want arms once more. . . . Everything beginning with the child's primer down to the last newspaper, every theatre and every movie, every billboard and every bare board, must be placed at the service of this great mission." [2] Yes, that is the genuine Nazi programme, and all who disagree, or are disqualified by their birth from agreeing, must be silenced. So the artists go into exile.

A civilisation progresses when its members desire to discover the truth and desire to express themselves creatively. The Nazis block progress down both these routes. The first is the route of science, and this pamphlet is not concerned with it, but I will quote from a speech which was made at the five hundred and fiftieth anniversary of the founding of the University of Heidelberg, by the Minister of Science and Education, as it expresses the governmental

[1] Thomas Mann: *The Coming Victory of Democracy.*
[2] Hitler, *Mein Kampf*, p. 715.

attitude neatly: "The charge of our enmity to science is true . . . if the complete absence of preconceptions and predispositions, unrestrained objectivity, are to be taken as characteristic of science. The old idea of science has gone for ever. The new science is entirely different from the idea of knowledge that found its value in an un-checked attempt to reach the truth." [1] The "check" implied by the Minister, is, of course, supplied by the State; it is for the State, not for the scientist, to define the scope of science.

The other route—the route of art—must be examined in more detail. It is a mistake to assume that the Nazis are against art and literature; they take more interest in them than we do, though from a harmful standpoint. I will paraphase an address given by Hitler in 1937, when he opened the House of German Art at Munich. It is full of falsities and crudities and cruelties, it is the sort of speech he makes every year, but it takes art seriously, which an Academy Banquet does not. The German threat is the more dangerous because she advertises a culture of her own.

The address begins by trouncing the Jews; with "their so-called artistic criticism" the Jews have muddled the public mind, and made out that art is international, and that it expresses the spirit of the age. They have put it on the level of fashions, which change yearly. But National-Socialist Germany demands—not modern art, but German art, which shall be, like the national spirit, eternal. "No doubt the Nation (das Volk) will pass, but so long as it exists it constitutes a stable pole in the whirling flux of time." And the artist must set up a monument to his na-

[1] *New York Times*, 30.6.36. Quoted by Lionel Trilling, in his *Matthew Arnold*.

tion, not to himself. The romantics (e.g., early nineteenth century painters like Runge) tried sincerely to express this "inwardly divined law of life". "But as for the degenerates, I forbid them to force their so-called experiences upon the public. If they do see fields blue, they are deranged, and should go to an asylum; if they only pretend to see them blue, they are criminals, and should go to prison. I will purge the nation of them, and let no one take part in their corruption—his day of punishment will come." [1]

Just as the scientist may not settle what experiments to make, so the artist may not settle how to express himself. In both cases an official intervenes. The official has never seen a field blue, and that decides, for all time, the colour of fields in pictures. The speech ends with the crack of a whip; the audience has been transported from the Art Gallery to the Concentration Camp; where it will be interned unless it minds its step, and enjoys what Hitler says is beautiful. This threat of a purge runs through all Nazi culture; the idea that one person may enjoy one thing and another another is intolerable to it. Sometimes the whip cracks comically, as at a circus, and we get a taste of the Teutonic sense of fun. For instance, Julius Streicher, the anti-Semite journalist, summoned all the reporters and editors of the Nuremburg press, many of whom were elderly men, and made them go on to a stage and do acrobatics on the tops of ladders. He did this because they had shown a tendency to be critical of the drama. Coming forward afterwards he explained that "whoever wishes to be understood by the people, must speak the people's language. Whoever wishes to appreciate an artist's accomplishment, must realise the labour and toil which are hidden

[1] Hitler: *Die Kunst ist in den Völkern begründet,* Munich 1937.

behind the accomplishment." [1] Streicher was carrying out
with jollity the instructions which had been issued in the
previous year by the Reich Propaganda Minister, Goebbels: in these the criticism of art, literature, music or
drama "as hitherto exercised" was sternly forbidden, and
"objective analysis and description" was to take its place,
and even then not to be practised without a special li-
cence.[2]

It is easy to laugh at all this garbage. But the people
who proclaim it have, unfortunately, the most powerful
army and air force in the world.

The Burning of the Books

The famous Burning of the Books is, as the Nazis wished
it to be, a symbol of their mentality. On the night of May
13th, 1933, 25,000 volumes were destroyed outside the
University of Berlin, in the presence of about 40,000 people. Some of the books were by Jews, others communist,
others liberal, others "unscientific" and all were "un-
German". It was for the government to decide what was
"un-German". There was an elaborate ritual. Nine her-
alds came forward in turn, and consigned an author with
incantations to the flames. For example, the fourth Herald
said: "Condemning the corrosion of the soul by the exag-
geration of the dangers of war! Upholding the nobility of
the human spirit! I consign to the flames the writings of
Sigmund Freud." The seventh Herald said: "Condemning
the literary betrayal of the World War soldier! Upholding
the education of our people in the spirit of reality! I
consign to the flames the writings of Erich Maria Re-

[1] *Fränkischen Kurier,* quoted in *De Telegraaf,* 7.3.37.
[2] Instructions dated 27.11.36.

marque!" [1] There were holocausts in the provinces too, and students were instructed to erect "pillars of infamy" outside their universities; the pillar should be "a thick tree-trunk somewhat above the height of a man", to which were to be nailed "the utterances of those who, by their participation in activities defamatory to character have forfeited their membership in the German nation". The reference to "character" is significant; "character", like "the soul", is always an opportunity for brutality. (One remembers the moral purges in which the Nazis have also indulged, and which have pleased a few foolish Mrs. Grundys over here; professing to purify the national character, they were actually directed against anyone whom the government disliked or wanted to rob, more particularly against the religious communities of the Roman Catholic Church.) The "Burning of the Books" heralded a systematic control of literature. Rosenberg, in his capacity of Commissioner for Philosophy and Education, created a bureau to look after the public libraries; existing stocks were to be overhauled, new purchases supervised.[2] Private lending libraries and secondhand bookshops were also purged. An official publication appears each month, and lists books "not to be sponsored"; eleven were on the list in the April number.[3]

Down with Goethe and Heine!

Two tiresome figures loomed from the nineteenth century past, and had to be dealt with: Goethe and Heine. Heine was the easier proposition, being a Jew, and also

[1] See *What Hitler Did to Us*, by Eva Lips (wife of the former director of the Museum of Ethnology, Cologne).

[2] *Berliner Börsen Zeitung*, 11.3.35.

[3] *Bücher-Künde*, April 1940.

possessed of certain admitted defects upon which critics could fasten. He is accordingly "the most baneful fellow that ever passed through German life . . . soul-devastating, soul-poisoning" and his *Buch der Lieder* "an unending series of sometimes not too bad, though sometimes just bungled varieties of irrelevant themes".[1] His lyric *Die Lorelei* still appears in text-books, but the name of its author is not given.

Goethe had to be treated with more respect than Heine, and so far as I know he has not been banned. But the Nazis rightly consider him their arch enemy and "Deutschland ohne Goethe" has been one of their rallying cries.

"In the decades to come, Goethe will be eclipsed, because he rejected the power of a type-forming ideal, and both in his life and his poetry refused to recognise the dictatorship of thought, without which a nation neither remains a nation nor will ever create a true commonwealth. Just as Goethe forbade his son to take part in the German War of Liberation . . . so, were he alive to-day, he would not be a leader in the struggle for the freedom . . . of our century." [2]

The shade of Goethe would scarcely quarrel with the above. He would not have become a Gauleiter. He did reject the "type-forming ideal", for he believed in variety. He did refuse to recognise the "dictatorship of thought", and if he could see his *Conversations with Eckermann* being pulped [3] he would observe a further example of it. Goethe was the nationalist who is ripe for supernationalism, the German who wanted Germany's genius to enrich the whole world. He is on our side. His spirit will re-arise when this madness and cruelty have passed.

[1] Adolf Bartels, *Geschïchte der Deutschen Literatur.*
[2] A. Rosenberg.
[3] Letter of Emil Ludwig in the *Neues Tagebuch* of Paris, 24.4.37.

Books have troubled the Nazis most, because of their tendency to comment upon contemporary life, even when they were written years ago. No government will ever make the State book-proof; Antigone still invokes the Unwritten Law against the totalitarianism of Creon; writers as diverse as Milton and Montaigne still insinuate themselves into the twentieth century, and remind it of freedom. Books are the more difficult to control, because their attack can be sideways as well as frontal; their direct message may be inoffensive, but their implications, or the way they are written, or that indefinable quality, their atmosphere, may slip into the reader's mind and put him against the National Socialist ideal. Burnings and bannings are therefore imperative, writers who show individuality must be shut up or shut out. The other arts cause less anxiety. In music, for instance, the criminals are fewer; Mendelssohn, Meyerbeer, Offenbach, Max Bruch, Mahler, Joachim from the past, Hindemith, Schönberg, Ernest Bloch, Toscanini in the present. Most of these are attacked because they are Jews. In the visual arts there is a longer list; Picasso and Klee are among the painters whose work has been banned, Erich Mendelssohn and Walter Gropius among the architects. Official art, as in Russia, tends to be academic and insipid; maidens among beech trees, colossal but unsuggestive nudes, classical porticoes, and behind them all the emptiness that haunted the faces of those Nazi soldiers and airmen.

WHAT IS GERMANY DOING TO EUROPE?

Germany's attitude towards the culture of occupied or conquered countries is inevitable: she is doomed to persecute them.

To begin with Czecho-Slovakia. Here, though cultural freedom was solemnly promised, she has suppressed whatever is likely to arouse emotion. Thus, though Czech music may be played as usual over the wireless, the folk songs may be only given instrumentally—not sung. Singing excites. Café owners have been arrested for allowing singing. Smetana's operas *Libuse* and *The Brandenburgers in Bohemia* have been banned; the first because it had a patriotic song by a mythical princess, the second because its title was too topical. The plays of Karel Capek may not be performed and according to some (though not all) accounts his writings have been suppressed. All school- and faculty-libraries have been forbidden to circulate books by Masaryk, Capek, Benes. School text-books have been revised and the Hussite period reduced to three sentences. The general line seems to be that of badgering and worrying and eviscerating; Czech culture is to survive as an æsthetic, not as a creative force. Naturally there are protests. The body of the poet K. H. Macha, who died a hundred years ago at Litornerice, was exhumed when that town was lost to the Germans after Munich, was brought by an immense concourse of people to lie in state at Prague. Then there was the protest of the Prague students, 120 of whom were killed. And—most touching of all—the protest of Karel Capek, who actually died of a broken heart, of sorrow.[1]

The Sudeten area is used for disseminating German influences all over the Protectorate. Last May was to be a "cultural month" during which the "creative forces of the homeland" could be forced upon the public, with the assistance of the "Strength through Joy" movement. The culmination was at Prague (alleged to be a German town),

[1] The above facts are taken from various well-documented pamphlets published by the American Friends of Czecho-Slovakia.

when Alfred Rosenberg was to speak on German Culture in War Time, so as to bring "the activities of the district into the closest connection with the rest of the Reich." [1] Germanisation is pushed through the schools and universities and public libraries; for instance, a subvention of 20,000 kroners was given to the German City Library at Olmütz, so that it might bring its stocks into line with the principles of the Reich.[2] It is evidently hoped that Czech culture will slowly fade away without giving too much trouble.

The fate of Polish culture has been more violent, since Poland is a conquered enemy; their conduct in Poland, rather than their conduct in Czecho-Slovakia, is the model which the Nazis would follow if they got over here. Observe how they treated the Jagellon University of Cracow (and then for "Cracow" put "Oxford"). Last November 170 professors and teachers were summoned by the chief of the Gestapo to the University Hall and informed that because they were continuing their work without Nazi permission they were under arrest. They were sent straight away to concentration camps in Germany, many of them to Sachsenhausen. Sixteen of them died, including Ignacy Chrzanowski, the leading authority on Polish literature. I know Cracow. I had friends in the university there, of whom I can get no news. They have welcomed me to their charming little flat overlooking the green boulevards, and shown me the marvellous fortress of the Wawel, half-Vatican, half-Kremlin in spirit, which towers against the curve of the Vistula. Owing to their kindness and hospitality, it has happened that "Cracow" has become for me the symbol of Nazi bullying on the continent, and I can hardly see

[1] *Die Zeit,* 21.4.40. I do not know how the festivities went.
[2] *Die Zeit,* 22.2.40.

the name without trembling with rage. This is only personal; other people will have other symbols, and no doubt more terrible ones. Nor is Cracow the only university in Poland to suffer; the professors at Warsaw and at Poznañ have been similarly treated.[1] The control of national culture is carried out in the usual Nazi way: for instance, the Governor General published on October 26 a decree providing that every book and periodical had to be submitted for authorisation before it was printed. And Germanisation is going ahead; an enormous German lending library has been started at Warsaw in the premises of the former Polish Central Library; "going through the rooms and seeing the endless rows of volumes, one is convinced that here a work of culture really has been created", a German visitor remarks.[2]

In Scandinavia, the Nazi problem is different. For the moment they want to conciliate. They have had some success in Norway; the novelist Knut Hamsun is reported to have advised his countrymen to accept their protection, and carried on the national betrayal begun by Major Quisling and the Bishop of Oslo. The younger Norwegian writers are furious with Hamsun and it is indeed an extraordinary decision, if the report be true; it shows what a strange view a writer, and a very great one, can take of his duty. From Denmark, there is little news; though in Copenhagen Karel Capek's play, *The Mother,* had to be taken off, and the première of *The Man Without a Soul* had to be cancelled; this was a play by the Swedish dramatist, Pär Lagerkvist, and its subject was dictatorship.

The policy in Holland seems also conciliatory. A Dutch correspondent writes to me: "The Germans are for the

[1] *Warschauer Zeitung*, 13.3.40.
[2] *Daily Telegraph*, 5.4.40.

moment trying to interfere as little as possible with Dutch
life, cultural life included. They are trying to persuade
our people that the invasion and occupation are no disasters. That this period of persuasion will be followed by
one of suppression is clear." He adds that none of the
reputable Dutch writers are pro-Nazi, whether of the older
or the younger generation.

I have no news about Belgium, and it is a nightmare to
speculate what is happening in France. France was, to my
mind, the light, the major light of the world, and for the
moment she is darkness. We have to go on alone.

WHAT WOULD GERMANY DO TO US?

What about us?

What would the Nazis do to our civilisation if they
won?

Perhaps we have data enough now to approach this
question.

Things are not perfect here, and it is cant to pretend
that they are; praise of British freedom must always raise
the questions of how much freedom, and of what sort of
freedom. During the present century, the writer, and the
artist generally, have worked under increasing disabilities;
the Law of Defamatory Libel hits them unfairly, so does
the Law of Obscene Libel, so do the Blasphemy Laws, so
does the Dramatic Censorship. And since last September,
conditions have become much worse, owing to regulations
judged necessary for the defence of the realm; publishers
and printers are terrified of handling anything which
might be thought disloyal, with the result that much original work and valuable comment is being stifled. This cannot be helped, and it is no use whining. But it is well to

remember that as soon as this war is won, people who care about civilisation will have to begin another war, a war inside England, for the restoration and extension of cultural freedom, and that neither our M.P.s nor our permanent officials nor the broadcasting authorities are likely to give us much assistance in the fight.

This proviso made, we can return to our immediate problem. Cultural conditions are not perfect here, but they are paradise compared with the conditions in Germany, and heaven compared with the conditions Germany would impose if she won. We see what she has done in her madness to her own children, we see what she is doing to neighbours whom she has no special reason to hate. What would she do to us, whom she has excellent reasons for hating?

Let me attempt a prophecy. The Press, the publishing and printing trades, the universities, and the rest of the educational system, the stage, and the films would be instantly controlled. The British Government (assuming one to exist) would be held responsible for their conduct, and punish them if they did anything which displeased Berlin. There would be complete remodelling, both in character and personnel, and most of the worthies who at present figure in *Who's Who* would disappear. In these respects, the methods adopted in Czecho-Slovakia and Poland would be followed and applied with the maximum of brutality; the joy of baiting Englishmen in England would be intoxicating. Germanisation would probably not be attempted. But the Gestapo and the rest of the occupying force would of course import such Nazi culture as was necessary for their mental sustenance, and we should have to pay heavily for German libraries and German schools.

The fate of individual writers would be hard. Those of

any eminence would be interned or shot. This, however painful to themselves, would not, it is true, be a blow to English literature, for by the time writers have become eminent they have usually done their best work. What would matter, what would be disastrous, is the intimidation of the younger writers—men and women in their twenties and thirties who have not yet had the chance of expressing themselves. The invaders would take care to frighten them or to cajole them. Forbidden to criticise their conquerors, forbidden to recall past glories, or to indulge that free movement of the mind which is helpful to the creative act, they would be confined to trivialities, or to spreading their masters' opinions. A bureau would be established, under English pro-Nazi writers, and licences to create or to comment would be issued, as in Germany by Goebbels, and withdrawn if independence was shown. Rebelliousness would mean death. I don't think I am prophesying wildly. It is only what is happening in Europe, and why should we get special terms? Nor am I accusing our enemies of any general hatred of culture. Like ourselves, they enjoy reading books or going to plays and films. They, too, want to be happy. But they dare not leave culture alone, because it is mixed up with thought and action. They are doomed to oppose it—just as it is their doom to oppose religion until Parsival (but will he ever be born?) comes along, and breaks the long sequence of their crimes.

The Case of Shakespeare

I do not believe that they would try to burn our national classics. The job would be too big. But a different orientation might be attempted in our schools, possibly centring round Shakespeare and Carlyle. Carlyle (if we ignore his belief that thought is stronger than artillery parks) certainly had something of the Nazi about him; he protests against Individualism and yet exalts the Hero; he despises Liberty, and holds that "the safeguard of Society lies not in the Constitution and the Laws, but in the strong bond of a uniform outlook." [1] Thus interpreted, Carlyle might be forced upon our young. The case of Shakespeare is more complicated. The Teutons have invested in him so heavily that they dare not, even under the present regime, sell out. But they feel worried, since we have invested too, and have been obliged to make Shakespeare into "the special case of a poet who is not affected by a war with England". He belongs (they assert) to an England which has vanished, and "when the great Nazi dramatist of the future comes, the goddess of victory will fly round his head, sun and wind stand at his back, as he looks at the enemy, he finds England, yet no longer the one from which Shakespeare sprang".[2] Shakespeare, like Carlyle, will be employed for our castigation and to our shame. And he will come as an alien. As for modern books, they might be destroyed if they were by Jews, or if they were in favour of liberalism; the fate of communist books would naturally depend upon the turns of the Russo-German pact. Even if nothing was done, our national mentality would change if we were conquered, and in directions which we cannot foresee: we should probably become secretive and find symbolical rallying points in books and plays and films, to which we should lend special emphasis and hysterical applause; so used the

[1] Theodor Deimel, *Carlyle und der Nationalsozialismus*, 1937.
[2] *Wille und Macht*, February 1940. The article, which is interesting, continues: "England's great poets to-day, Bridges and Masefield, shun all things national, patriotic and racial. Sheriff, author of the best war-play, has nothing of the spirit of Percy Hotspur, Wilfrid Owen groans forth incomparable war poetry, but it rends the heart without healing it."

Italians to applaud Verdi in far-off days, because the initials of "Vittorio Emanuele, Re d'Italia" formed his name and spelt liberty to them. The Nazis would be on the lookout for such twisted demonstrations; they have had to deal with them elsewhere, and understand them well. Of one thing we may be certain whether we are readers or writers: if we tried to go on as we are, we should be punished.

Conclusion

Much as I long for peace, I cannot see how we are to come to terms with Hitler. For one thing, he never keeps his word, for another he tolerates no way of looking at things except his own way. A peace which was the result of a Nazi victory would surely not differ much from a Nazi war. Germans would no longer be killed, but they would go on killing others, until no one survived to criticise them. In the end they might achieve world-domination, and feel secure enough to practise the arts and institute a culture. But what sort of culture would it be? The imagination reels. What would they have to work with? For you cannot go on destroying lives and living processes without destroying your own life. If you continue to be greedy and dense, if you make power and not understanding your god, if, as a French friend puts it, you erect "une pyramide d'appétits à base de stupidité", you atrophy the impulse to create. Creation is disinterested. Creation is passionate understanding. Creation lies at the heart of civilisation like fire at the heart of the earth. Around it are gathered its cooler allies—criticism, the calm use of the intellect—informing the mass and moulding it into shape. The brain is not everything—the Nazis are perfectly right there—but no one can insult the brain without becoming sterile and cruel.

We know their cruelty. We should see their sterility if their orgy of destruction were to stop, and they turned at their Führer's orders to the production of masterpieces.

In this difficult day when so many of us are afraid (anyhow I am; afraid; not jittery); in this day when so many brave plans have gone wrong and so many devices jammed; in this day when decency has retired to the democracies, and the democracies are in peril: it is a comfort to remember that violence has so far never worked. Even when it conquers, it fails in the long run. This failure may be due to the Divine Will. It can also be ascribed to the strange nature of Man, who refuses to live by bread alone, and alone among the animals has attempted to understand his surroundings.

"I prayed, and understanding was given to me: I called upon God, and the spirit of Wisdom came to me . . . All good things together came to me with her, and innumerable riches in her hands. And I rejoiced in them all because Wisdom goeth before them; and I knew not that she was the mother of them."

This rejoicing will not be for our generation. Whatever the outcome of the war, we are in for bad times. But there are moments when each of us, however feeble, can feel within himself the strong hopes of the human race, and see beyond his personal death its renaissance, and the restoration of delight.

THE CROOKED CROSS

By

DR. A. S. DUNCAN-JONES

Dean of Chichester

THE CROOKED CROSS

FOR those who had eyes to see, the Nazi attack on the Churches was the earliest and also the clearest exposure of the true character of National Socialism. Though the treatment of the Jews was more shocking by reason of its brutality and sadism, this cruel campaign revealed less of the inner nature of the forces that had climbed to power at the beginning of 1933. Anti-Semitism fitted in naturally with the racial doctrine which was the chief instrument of Hitler and his associates for reviving and solidifying the national ambitions.

Anti-Semitism had a negative as well as a positive advantage from Hitler's point of view. The very violence of the outbreak would lull to sleep suspicions aroused by other aspects of the Nazi spirit. Other nations might well feel that, while the Nazi energies were so fully occupied with the congenial task of persecuting these helpless people, it would leave them little time or inclination to become a threat to peoples dwelling outside the borders of Germany, and this consoling, if cynical, conclusion would be confirmed by the belief that those who were racially akin to the Germans had nothing to fear from the national resurgence. Events proved that these calculations were not without foundation. The persecution of the Jews, though it deeply shocked men and women of all countries who think first in terms of ordinary humanity, had very little effect on diplomats or statesmen.

The attack on the Churches was in a different category. For this no racial excuses could be advanced. The strongly national tinge running through all Church life in Germany made such an outbreak astonishing. That the Churches should find themselves in opposition on various points to a free-thinking liberal Government, like the Weimar regime, was intelligible; though, in fact, the relations between the Churches and the Republic were far more friendly than might have been expected. But that a movement which claimed to restore the national spirit, to introduce a lost social order, and to be the bitter foe of "Godless Communism", should find itself in opposition to the Churches was indeed a matter for surprise. The answer from Berlin was quickly forthcoming. What appeared to be persecution was not such really. The parsons were interfering in politics. The actions of the State were not of a persecuting character. They were merely defensive. If the parson would stick to his job he would not get into trouble. This explanation was easily accepted by many in other countries, who disliked the notion that religion had anything to do with public affairs. There were indeed some who accepted this piece of propaganda until war broke out.

Once again politicians were put off the scent by the reflection that a theological and ecclesiastical conflict must be a purely internal matter, with which they had nothing to do. Though in one sense this judgment was entirely correct—obviously no intervention was called for—yet this unexpected phenomenon had much to teach the statesmen and diplomats, if they had given their attention to it in time. The truth was that the attack on the Church conveyed a political lesson of the first importance. It revealed the Nazi party as a gang determined to impose their power on their fellow-Germans without scruple, and thereby exploded the supposed racial basis of the Nazi philosophy. The attack also brought to the front the implications of the *Weltanschauung*—the word repeated *ad nauseam* by the fervent young Nazis. The *Weltanschauung* was a view of life and of the world, demanding the loyalty given to a religion, and endowed with a missionary enthusiasm that recognised no frontiers.

The False Messiah

The real power of the National Socialist Movement in Germany can only be understood when it is recognised as a form of religion. Every substantial political movement has about it an element of faith. But ordinary political movements in Western Europe do not claim the complete devotion, body and mind, of their adherents. This is precisely what National Socialism does. Nazism and Communism have this fundamental totalitarian characteristic in common. They can brook no rival loyalty. As Karl Barth said in his lecture to the Swiss Evangelical Church in December, 1938, "National Socialism is a religious institution of salvation. . . . It is impossible to understand National Socialism, unless we see it in fact as a new Islam, its myth as a new Allah, and Hitler as this new Allah's Prophet." The comparison is apt. Dr. Ley, the leader of the Labour Front, has said, "I believe on this earth in Adolf Hitler alone. I believe in one Lord God who made me and guides me, and I believe that this Lord God has sent Adolf Hitler to us." There is, however, a profound difference between Mohammedanism and Hitlerism. Mohammed was a prophet who believed in a transcendent God, before whom he bowed and by whom he would be judged. Hitler's God is immanent in himself; he is a demi-God, not a prophet. The Divine is for him merely the power which enables him to do more efficiently what he wants.

The secret of the success of National Socialism lies precisely in the religious, mystical element, symbolised in the Swastika. The terrible *débâcle* that immediately followed the last war left masses of the German people eager for redemption, for a reversal of their fate, and passionately longing for some star to which to hitch their waggon. Reason does not play the part in the German mentality that it does in the French or English. The great German philosophers have been half mystics. The young German especially was looking for something romantic and mysterious that would hold out the prospect of a speedy millennium which would save him from his fear of standing alone by planting him in a national community, and would give him the assurance that defeat would be reversed. Into this Messianic mood the dervish-like ragings of Hitler, with their call for blind obedience, fitted admirably. The Germans do everything to excess. There is, as Coleridge (who admired them), said, a nimiety, a too-muchness about the Germans. The German people had fallen into an unreasonable excess of depression. Hitler raised them into an equally unreasonable excess of exaltation and defiance. Hitler had felt the pulse of the common man. He knew what he was doing. His instinct was uncannily correct.

Hitler's aims are fundamentally political. They are the possession of power for the German people, and for himself, as the controller and representative of the German people. At the moment he has achieved considerable success. His power over the German people is complete, and he has extended his control over a number of other peoples. This success has been due to his clear perception that physical force by itself will not achieve power. It must go hand in hand with kindling ideas. The sword needs propaganda as its ally. "Any attempt to contend with a World View by material force will fail in the end, unless the struggle takes the form of an attack on behalf of a new spiritual outlook. Only in the struggle of two World Views can the weapon of brute force, persistently and ruthlessly employed, bring about a decision favourable to the party it supports." Philosophical ideas are not sufficient. The common man does not live by philosophy but by faith. "Faith," he said, "is harder to shake than reason."

Hitler's Promises

Thus Hitler himself bears witness to the fact that he is engaged in a conflict of religions. How much he really believes in the doctrines of blood and soil it would be hard to say. What is certain is that he correctly gauged the situation, when he saw the necessity of providing some kind of religious, philosophical, mystical spell to rally the dim multitudes to his political purposes. From the first he had recognised that he must get control of the Churches, because they represented a spiritual force that would otherwise challenge his supreme mastery of the minds of men. Since he did not wish to arouse unnecessary antagonism in the early stages he had to conceal his ultimate aims until his power was thoroughly established. He would need the support of members of the Churches and of that larger number of Germans that respected, even if they did not practise, the Christian religion.

Hitler therefore in *Mein Kampf* took up the position that a political leader should not confuse his task with that of the religious reformer. Any other position would, he said, lead to catastrophe in Germany. Thus, when he first came into power, he made a bid for Christian support by his ferocious denunciations of "Godless Bolshevism" and by a vague, but specious, promise to uphold the Churches. In his speech to the Reichstag on March 23, 1933, Hitler said, "The National Government sees in the two Christian Confessions most vital factors in the survival of our nationality. Their rights will not be touched. The National Government will accord and secure to the Christian Confessions the influence that is due to them in schools and education." This piece of propaganda was highly successful. There was much in the current Nazi teaching to raise doubts. This declaration lulled to sleep many who were only too anxious to accept the new saviour. One of the first acts of the new regime was designed still further to allay any fear of a conflict between National Socialism and Christianity. On July 20, 1933, a Concordat between the German Government and the Vatican was signed at Rome by Cardinal Pacelli and Franz von Papen. By this striking act Hitler wished to appear in the light of a more effective supporter of Christian traditions than the Weimar Government had been.

German or Christian

But there can be no doubt about Hitler's own personal attitude. It has been made clear by two separate witnesses who have had first-hand opportunities of knowing his mind. They are both men who have been disappointed in Hitler, but for entirely opposite reasons. For Kurt Luedecke (*I Knew Hitler*, p. 465) Hitler is a traitor to the true radicalism of National Socialism. Dr. Hermann Rauschning, on the other hand, is a conservative, who abandoned

Hitler because he was alarmed at the anarchical nihilism which he believes to be its inner essence. Luedecke reports that Hitler said "with passionate energy", "Of course, I, myself, am a heathen to the core". In Dr. Rauschning's hearing Hitler said (*Hitler Speaks,* p. 57), "One is either a German or a Christian. You cannot be both." Hitler shrewdly recognises that even a Unitarian view of Jesus Christ is dangerous, because it implies a belief in immortality. "We don't want people who keep one eye on the life in the hereafter. We need free men who feel and know that God is in themselves."

Both writers also agree that Hitler avoided an open attack upon the Churches, not only because he did not wish to become involved in complications, but also because he was convinced that the Churches had lost all life and would wither away when the mass enthusiasm of the new fanatical nationalism got into the saddle. The young would be captured by the dynamic appeal to believe only in themselves, in Germany and above all in the Leader, and to secure by this means a domination, first of their own people, and then of the whole world. Hitler's method for dealing with possible opponents, whether it be in the national or in the international sphere, is the same. He aims at the formation of sympathetic groups, at undermining resistance by a mixture of promises, flattery, blackmail and terror. It is characteristic of his mentality that he believes there are few men who cannot be won over by the hope of reward or the fear of pain.

The Nazi attack on the Protestant Church in Germany provided a perfect example of that method of disintegration from within, which Hitler has since practised with such success in other fields.

The Nazi Faith

The fundamental tenet of the Nazi faith is the sacredness of the German race, which, though called by God to rule the world, is attacked and hemmed in by the powers of evil, incarnate in the Jews, and in a whole group of grasping, jealous powers who combined in diabolic international systems for the sole purpose of defeating the Divine purpose. Like St. George, he, Hitler, has been raised up to deliver the Chosen People from these foul adversaries. This is what the Swastika stands for. This is the religion of the Crooked Cross. We have compared it to Mohammedanism. Like Mohammedanism it is very largely borrowed from the Bible. It is a fantastic imitation of Judaism, with the God of Holiness and Love left out. An illuminating statement of this German Faith is to be found in a Kiel High School paper published in 1935:—

"We believe that God has revealed Himself to us in our German blood and German consciousness, in our German home and German history. That is our German Faith. We regard the word 'heathen' as an honourable term, not as a reproach. We are proud of our German Faith, our Northern Heathenism.

"We cannot take our religious faith from the Jews any more. We recognise no international religion of humanity because People and Races are different. Therefore we German Heathen want no more Jewish foreign religion in Germany. We do not believe in the Holy Ghost any more. We believe in the Holy Blood.

"The foundation of the Jewish-Christian teaching is the dogma of Original Sin. The foundation of our heathen feeling for life is a belief in the value of healthy Blood.

"Whoever has thoroughly grasped the thought of Race

must reject the Jewish foreign religion in every form, Catholic or Evangelical, German Church or German Christian.

"We believe in God, the inscrutable, mysterious power of Fate, which we experience in Blood and Consciousness, Home and Universe."

So far as the Protestant Church was concerned, Hitler thought that he would have an easy task. His upbringing under Roman Catholic auspices left him deeply imbued with two ideas. Though he hated the Roman Catholic Church and thought its days were numbered, he retained a profound respect for the secular grandeur of an institution which had lasted two thousand years. He felt he had something to learn from its astuteness, its knowledge of human nature, its political sense. At the same time he shared the contempt for Protestantism to be found among the more unthinking of Roman Catholics. He attributed Bismarck's failure in the *Kulturkampf* of the '70s to the fact that, as a Protestant, he did not understand a real Church. Just because the Protestants did not know what a Church was they would soon submit to pressure. The Protestant parsons would cause no difficulty. "They are insignificant people, submissive as dogs, and they sweat with embarrassment when you talk to them. They have neither a religion that can be taken seriously nor a great position to defend like Rome. They will betray anything for the sake of their little jobs and incomes."

Hitler relied on the disintegration wrought in the Protestant Church by the absorption of sceptical and critical ideas during the last half century. "Do you think," Dr. Rauschning heard him say, "these liberal priests, who have no longer a belief, only an office, will refuse to preach *our* God in their Churches? I can guarantee that, just as they have made Haeckel and Darwin, Goethe and Stefan Georg the prophets of their Christianity, so they will replace the Cross with our Swastika."

"German Christians"

One of the first tasks of the Nazis, after their seizure of power, was to find some means of grafting the Swastika on to the Evangelical Church. Hitler was astute enough to see that this must be done from within. He elaborately dissociated himself from the affair. "I am a Catholic," he said, when I asked him in July, 1933, whether he wished to form a State Church, "I have no position in the Protestant Church." All he was doing was to protect it (as rulers had always done) from falling into chaos. The truth, of course, was that the only element making for chaos was the violent minority which was endeavouring to "nazify" the Evangelical Church.

The declared aim of this minority, who called themselves "German Christians", was a united Church, a People's Church and a Church racially German, a Church founded on blood and soil, a Church that rejected altogether the idea of a Christian world citizenship.

The demand for a united Church was part of the general Nazi scheme for bringing every activity of German life under the complete control of the Party, a process called by the ambiguous name "co-ordination" (*Gleichschaltung*). Since the one Party State itself was the submissive servant of the small group of adventurers who led it, the one Party State meant a State in which Hitler, Göring, Goebbels, Himmler and Hess would have at their mercy the life and liberty of every citizen of the country. They are men without morals and without mercy.

Since their character was well-known amongst educated

people in Germany, the demand for a united Church had to be narrowly examined by those responsible for the Church. The argument in favour of a united Protestant Church was from one point of view difficult to resist. For more than a century the German people had been striving to gather into one the congeries of kingdoms, duchies and principates which was the legacy of the Holy Roman Empire of the German People. Bismarck's Empire of blood and iron had been able to achieve a federation. The post-War changes had swept away the kings and princes, but in many ways the particularist spirit remained. Of this particularist spirit one of the most evident remaining signs were the twenty-eight separate Churches (*Landeskirchen*) which still existed. Moreover German Protestants were divided into Lutherans and Calvinists. The move for unity excited wide sympathy. The question was, How was that unity to be obtained and to be maintained? The proper Church answer was, By voluntary action and by consent.

Reichsbishop

But this was not at all to the mind of the German Christians. Their object in pressing so hard for a unified Church was to make it easier to imbue the whole body with Nazi principles, to impose upon it the *Führerprinzip,* and so to make the Church an instrument for the promotion of Hitler's ambitions for Germany. They demanded a Reichsbishop. At this point there emerged a Pastor Ludwig Mueller, a naval chaplain, unknown to fame, but in the confidence of Hitler.

The constitutional representatives of the Evangelical Church were Dr. Kapler, Dr. Marahrens, Bishop of Hanover, and Dr. Hesse, a Calvinist from Elberfeld. With

Pastor Mueller, they drew up a constitution for the united Church which accepted the office of Reichsbishop. What the Church leaders refused to do was to choose Mueller as the first Reichsbishop. They put forward Pastor von Bodelschwingh, a man of deep piety and wide pastoral experience. Their choice was confirmed by the Churches. The fury of the "German Christians" knew no bounds. As a result of their agitation Hitler intervened, though keeping himself in the background. On his instructions a lawyer, Dr. Jaeger, was appointed State Commissar with plenary power for the Church of Prussia, much the largest of the German Protestant Churches.

Such action was wholly illegal. When Jaeger first attempted to put the Church under police supervision and dismissed pastors without trial a violent opposition was created. In order to silence it a synod was elected in which a "German Christian" majority was obtained by Nazi party propaganda, assisted by Hitler himself. Mueller's appointment was afterwards confirmed, when this Synod met at Wittenberg in September. The whole procedure is characteristic of Hitler's methods. He has always attempted to cover his most arbitrary acts by a cloak of constitutional procedure, in order to satisfy the orderly instinct so deep in the German mind.

The Confessional Movement

The elaborate sham by which the Reichsbishop was imposed on the Evangelical Church only deceived those who wished to be deceived. There were many pastors who, in no way accepting the Nazi ideology, were yet swept off their feet by the national resurgence. But, by this time, a group of pastors had been formed, determined to uphold the purity of the Gospel and the spiritual independence of the Church. Hitler, whose knowledge of religious matters was of the most superficial, had made a bad mistake when he relied on the old Lutheran spirit of subservience to the State and the debilitating effects of "liberalism" in theology to make easy his task of bringing the Protestant Churches into line. Great changes had been wrought in the world of Protestant theology. The War had revealed the weakness of a religion that was mere moralism. Sincere Christians had been thrown back on the Living God, the God of the Bible; criticism had done a useful work in bringing to the front the apocalyptic element in the New Testament; and, not least important, the separation of the Church from the State introduced by the Weimar Republic had taught the younger generation of Protestant pastors to rely on the inherent spiritual power of the Church itself, now that the Prince, the Summus Episcopus, had been withdrawn.

It thus happened—most providentially—that, when the challenge of the Nazi dogmas burst upon the Church, they were confronted within the Evangelical Church itself by a powerful group, prepared to take their stand with equal determination on the unchanging dogmas of the Christian Church, contained in the historic Confessions of Faith. Their insistence on the Confessions of Faith led to the opposition becoming known as "the Confessionals". The controversy raged round two points, the nature and constitution of the Church and the Christian doctrine of man. To the claim of the secular power to impose a spiritual dictator in the person of the Reichsbishop they opposed the spiritual independence of the Church and its right to fashion its own government. The government of the Church, they maintained, is not a mere matter of convenience, but part of its spiritual essence. They also rejected the attempt to limit Church offices to those of "Aryan" stock; the doctrines of blood and soil were in flat contradiction to the universality of the Christian revelation and to the redemption offered to men of every race through the Blood of Jesus Christ. The Reichsbishop promulgated—on his own authority—a "muzzling order" forbidding pastors to introduce into their sermons any matter of Church controversy or to write books or pamphlets thereon, under pain of suspension from their office and the loss of one-third of their income.

The so-called law was categorically rejected by four thousand Confessional pastors who had formed themselves into an Emergency League (*Notbund*). The Confessional Front contained within itself different groups or tendencies. There were the younger pastors, men like Martin Niemöller, who had come under the influence of the revival of a positive Christianity. Many of them were Calvinists, but many were Lutherans; all owed something to the fearless proclamation of the supremacy of God by the Swiss prophet, Karl Barth. At the other end of the Front, so to speak, was the more conservative wing represented by the Lutheran bishops of Hanover, Bavaria and Württemberg, Dr. Marahrens, Dr. Meiser and Dr. Wurm. The more definite Confessionals were for the most to be found in the largest of the provincial Churches, that of Prussia, the constitutional organisation of which had been destroyed by Reichsbishop Mueller. The other bishops had contrived to preserve their Churches intact, and they were all strong Lutherans. For both these reasons they were more inclined to attempt a *modus vivendi* with the State.

A Drastic Step

For months the controversy swayed from side to side. Sometimes the Reichsbishop seemed to be willing to reach a reasonable solution. But whenever he did so, something always upset the arrangements. And there is no doubt that leading forces in the Nazi Party were furtively at work, using the "German Christians" as an instrument to prevent anything that would promote an independent Church, uncontrolled by Nazi ideology. This pressure, exercised through the official Church Government only, had the effect of welding more closely the Confessional Forces. At Barmen in May, 1934, they held a great Synod at which the whole German Evangelical Church was represented, Lutherans, Reformed and United. It declared that Mueller's Church Government had forfeited any claim to be the constitutional government of the Church, because it had betrayed the principles of the Gospel, and had attempted to subordinate the Word of God to secular powers who were claiming to be the instruments of a new revelation. The Synod took a drastic step; it drew up plans for the creation of a new and true Church government, and appointed a Council of Brethren to be the nucleus of such a government. By this action what had been the Confessional Movement became the Confessional Church.

The Reichsbishop counter-attacked in the Autumn by holding a so-called National Synod which included only reliable Nazis. The chief act of the Synod was the promulgation of an oath requiring every minister to swear to be true and obedient to the leader of the German People and State, Adolf Hitler, and to accept conscientiously all the orders of Mueller's Church Government. Mueller's next step was to issue decrees bringing the independent

Churches of Württemberg under his control. Bishop Wurm and Bishop Meiser both protested vigorously and were placed under arrest in their own houses. This action caused strong public protests both in Württemberg and Bavaria, and only served to show how popular the bishops were with their flocks. Dr. Jaeger, the lawyer who was the real power behind the Reichsbishop, thereupon removed Bishop Meiser from his office. With every fresh aggression on the part of the Church Ministry the popularity of the two redoubtable bishops increased by leaps and bounds. A mass demonstration of ten thousand people gathered on the Adolf Hitler Platz at Nuremberg to support Dr. Meiser. Their case was taken up throughout Germany.

The Reich Confessional Synod met in October at Dahlem, where Pastor Niemöller's parish was, and drew up a statement demanding that the Reich Government should cease to interfere with the Church. The combination of this firm action with the popular enthusiasm in South Germany, and the fact that important German Christians began to go over to the Confessional side had a remarkable effect. Dr. Jaeger was forced to resign, while the Reichsbishop retired into the background. Though he kept his title and his stipend, he ceased to be of any importance. Thus the first round of the conflict between the Party and the Church, in which the Nazis attempted to disintegrate the Church from within, ended with a defeat. The Evangelical Church had shown that it had an unexpected spiritual power.

The Old Gods

The set-back encouraged the Confessionals to take a bolder line, but it also made the Nazis more determined to get the Church under control. The Provisional Church

Government published a careful statement on February 21, 1935, warning the members of the Church against the new heathenism which had appeared with the declared object of fashioning a new type of man. In it the orthodox Protestant leaders—who understood very clearly where they stood and what it was that threatened them—set forth with precision the religion which the Nazis are promoting as a substitute for Christianity. The unbridgeable gulf between the Cross and the Crooked Cross stands out starkly.

In this new religion they said the old German gods reappeared—with a difference! Odin was now regarded as the symbol of those primitive forces of the soul of the Nordic man which still lived as he had done five thousand years ago. As the Eternal Wanderer he is the symbol of the Nordic soul ever seeking and pushing forward. In this new religion the relations between God and man are turned upside down. Man creates God in his image. He says, "If I did not exist, God would not exist." "The God whom we honour, would not exist, if our soul and blood did not exist." "I am the origin of myself in my eternal and my temporal life." "The Christian Churches are a monstrous travesty of the simple and glad message that the Kingdom of Heaven is within us." As a consequence the Old Testament must be discarded as a book of religion, and whatever in the New does not fit in with this Nordic faith. There must be no more sermons about the Lamb of God.

As the Confessional leaders pointed out, such a religion radically rejected the notion that the Bible contained a Divine Revelation and substituted for it the Voice of the Divine in the Blood, in the vitality of the Race, in the rhythm of nature and the evolution of history. Thus the God in which it believed was not personal but pantheist, naturalistic and ultimately atheist. Since faith was derived

from the Blood, everything racially foreign must be removed from religion. Consequently Paul could only be
regarded as a corrupter of the "pure Jesus teaching", and
a mere Jewish rabbi. The only sin known to the new
religion is a sin against "the Blood". The need for divine
Grace is removed, and the Cross becomes the sign not of
victory but of collapse. The principle of honour must replace the Christian idea of love, which is but another name
for a weak humanitarianism.

The Confessional leaders pointed out, with quiet irony,
that this body of ideas was merely a development (though
a very perverse one) of those "liberal" and Freemason conceptions which the Nazis professed to find so loathsome.
They called upon their people to choose whether they
would revere the God and Father of the Lord Jesus Christ
or this other God. They could not do both. The memorandum also appealed to the Government for perfect freedom
to uphold this faith and to controvert those errors, which
were flooding the Press, the theatre and even the schools,
with Government encouragements.

This bold challenge was a clarion call. Seven hundred
pastors who read the manifesto were either arrested or put
under house arrest and five thousand more were warned
by the Secret Police not to read it. It was thus made clear
that the new heathenism was the official religion of the
Third Reich. In order to press this point home a new
law was promulgated, transferring all Church disputes
from the courts of justice to a bureau of the Ministry of
Interior.

The State Demands

The struggle between the Evangelical Church and the
Nazi regime entered on a new phase in July, 1935. The

office of Reich Minister for Church Affairs was created, and a Herr Kerrl, a lawyer from the Prussian Ministry of Justice, only in the loosest sense a Churchman, was made the first minister. Henceforward it was plain that the Government intended to assume control over the Church. Kerrl had not been long in office before he issued a decree which established this control in the most complete manner. "The Reich Minister for Church Affairs is empowered, for the restoration of orderly conditions in the German Evangelical Church and the Regional Evangelical Churches, to issue ordinances with binding legal force."

Herr Kerrl's dictatorship was marked by a continuance of the methods which had been used by the Reichsbishop, the methods of profuse expressions of good will, accompanied by threats and diversified by violent and illegal action, which are characteristic of the Nazi mind. At first Kerrl let some of the pastors out of prison. (It is important to bear in mind that from 1934 onwards there never was a time when there were not pastors in prison without any attempt at legal trial.) His new plan for restoring order to the harassed Evangelical Church turned out to be a series of committees for the different regional Churches at the head of which was placed a Reich Committee. A much respected Churchman, Dr. Zoellner, was appointed chairman of the Reich Committee.

A new gleam of hope seemed to appear and many of the moderate Confessionals showed themselves ready to co-operate for the sake of peace. The more far-sighted, known as the Dahlem group, of whom Pastor Niemöller was the leader, were doubtful from the first. They were suspicious of organisations which ultimately had no Church authority, but only that of the State, and they refused to serve on them. On the other hand the committees that were formed in Württemberg and Bavaria were wholly Confessional, because "German Christians" were a negligible factor in these Churches; and these committees strongly criticised Dr. Zoellner, because the first appeal had not only affirmed the Confessional basis of the Church but "the National Socialist development of the people on the basis of Race, Blood and Soil". This was as good as saying that no one could be a Churchman who did not also accept the Nazi ideology.

Dr. Zoellner, whose good faith nobody questioned, was soon in difficulties with the committees. But it was not the Confessionals who caused him trouble. In a number of provincial Churches "German Christian" bishops had been appointed during the Mueller-Jaeger regime even though they represented only a small minority of the pastors and parishes. The committees wished them to resign as a first step to appeasement. This a number of them absolutely refused to do. After an interview with Herr Hitler, Kerrl strongly supported them in their refusal, thus revealing again the covert influence of the Führer behind the scenes.

It was not long before Herr Kerrl instituted sharper attacks on the Confessional Church. The first step was the confiscation of the trustee funds of the Church by the secret police; the next was an order requiring all writings multigraphed for distribution to be submitted to censorship before being sent out. Printing had been forbidden for a considerable time. But the Confessionals had created a very thorough and ingenious system for keeping in touch with their members by the use of typescript and manifolding. Kerrl next proceeded to deny to all Church associations or groups the right to exercise executive or administrative functions, such as the appointment of pastors, the examination and ordination of theological candidates, making collections, or holding synods. The meaning of these orders was plain: they were designed to paralyse the "Provisional Church Government" (*Vorläufige Leitung*). The Confessional Church refused to pay any attention to what they regarded as entirely illegal action.

A new and more vigorous Provisional Church Administration was formed in the spring of 1936 which included Pastor Niemöller, Dr. Boehm and Pastor Albertz.

The new Provisional Church Government very soon took a bold and determined initiative to test the real mind of the Nazi Government. In all that had happened so far, as has been pointed out, the Führer kept well in the background. The Confessional leaders had to meet the criticism that they were unduly suspicious of Kerrl, whose intentions were, it was asserted, really benevolent. There was only one way in which the whole situation could be cleared up, and that was to appeal directly to Hitler himself.

Questions to the Führer

Pastor Niemöller and his colleagues in the Provisional Church Administration understood that secrecy was essential. If they tried to put the Führer in the dock publicly, their object would not be achieved. Ways were found therefore to despatch to Hitler a memorandum which asked him searching questions. Had the attempt to dechristianise the German people, which was being so vigorously pursued, the co-operation of responsible statesman, or was it merely permitted? Were Goebbels and Rosenberg authorised to interpret "Positive Christianity" in a way that deprived it of all meaning? Were the attacks of party officials on the Christian Faith authorised by the Government? Why was the Church not allowed freely and publicly to answer these attacks?

The Confessional Pastors have often been slightingly spoken of, and not only in Germany—because, as it was said, they were only interested in parsons' problems and not in broad human questions. The memorandum to Hitler disposes of that charge. Not content with pleading for freedom to uphold their religious faith, they boldly criticised the regime in two fundamental respects. The Evangelical Christian, they said, was gravely injured in his loyalty by the existence of concentration camps in a State claiming to be founded on law, and by the power given to the Secret Police to take action against individuals without any process of law. They also asked Hitler directly whether he wished to accept the semi-divine position of a kind of mediator between God and the Peoples, which was freely accorded to him in certain quarters. The memorandum became public property, probably by Nazi action, and no reply ever came from Hitler. But the conflict was much accentuated. Many Germans who had very little idea of the acuteness of the struggle had it brought home to them, and pressure on the Church increased. Baldur von Schirach intensified his efforts to obtain complete control of the youth of Germany. Herr Rust, the Minister of Education, closed the Theological School at Elberfeld. The Church Committees were in the final stages of collapse. Dr. Zoellner and the Reich Church Committee resigned on February 12, 1937, on the ground that Kerrl made their task impossible by constant interference whenever—in the interest of order—they found it necessary to take action against "German Christians". Kerrl replied in a speech which made the situation perfectly plain. "There has now arisen a new authority concerning what Christ and Christianity really is. This new authority is Adolf Hitler."

Pastor Niemöller

The failure of the Church committees showed that there was no hope of reducing the Evangelical Church to the control of the Party by any method that pretended, with whatever camouflage, to have a Church character. More direct action was needed. The only way was to attack the parsons in their persons and their property. The latter Kerrl instituted by setting up Finance Departments which could regulate the terms of service of all Church officials. This was followed by a wave of arrests. Some five hundred pastors found themselves in prison cells for longer or shorter periods.

At last, on July 1, 1937, the Party stretched out its hand to seize the man for whom Hitler had the bitterest, quite personal, hatred, Martin Niemöller. It was not till the following February that he was brought to trial. The former submarine officer, who became a pastor after the World War, had struck the imagination of the world by the courage, the simplicity, the forthrightness of his defence of the freedom of religion in Germany, an impression all the stronger because it was known that he was an ardent patriot who had even voted National Socialist, and, as late as 1933, had preached a sermon applauding the national resurgence. He now stood before a judge charged with abuse of the pulpit for political purposes in accordance with an old law that Bismarck (grim irony) had concocted as a weapon against the Roman Catholics in his unsuccessful *Kulturkampf*. It was a tribute to the persistence of the concept of justice, even under the Nazi regime, that the

Special Court passed a sentence which would have allowed him to go free. No less clear a proof of the fact that in the Nazi State justice in the end is merely Hitler's will, was afforded by the seizure of Niemöller by the Gestapo as he was about to leave the court and his re-incarceration in a concentration camp where he has languished ever since. Though he has not suffered the physical barbarities meted out to some other pastors, only a stout heart and a profound faith could have sustained for so long a man by nature boundlessly active and energetic.

In his last sermon he had said, "We have no more thought of using our own power to escape the arm of the authorities than had the Apostles of old. No more are we ready to keep silence at man's behest when God commands us to speak. For it is, and must remain the case, that we must obey God rather than man".

This was the spirit that animated all the Confessional pastors, whose names are less known to fame. As the months wore on during 1938 and the early part of 1939 and the preparations for war became more and more intense in Germany, the pressure on all independent thought in the Evangelical Church increased. Attempts were made by Kerrl acting as the Government of the Church to impose on pastors a new oath of personal loyalty to the Führer; the leadership of the Confessional Church was paralysed by orders forbidding them to meet; and a law was promulgated by Dr. Werner in April, 1939, enabling the president of any provincial Church to remove any pastor from one parish to another and to allow German Christian minorities to set up a pastor in any parish where the lawful pastor was not sufficiently Nazi. In July a regulation was issued by Dr. Werner for the spiritual guidance of the provincial Churches which made the Nazi *Weltan-*

schauung obligatory for all members of the Evangelical Church. For Germans, he said, Christianity can only be understood within the boundaries of people and race.

Despite enormous difficulties, many of the Confessional pastors went on with their spiritual work wherever possible, undeflected, though the organisation of the Confessional Church had practically become non-existent.

The Church in War

Since the shadow of war has enveloped the German people few details that throw any light on the Church conflict can be descried. A tendency to concentrate on the national struggle manifested itself. The constraints of war, both in the spiritual and in the material sphere, have caused the cessation of all opposition to the regime for the time being. This is intelligible. What the future holds no man can say. It is difficult to believe that the frightful loss and suffering imposed on the German people in a totally unnecessary war will not in some way produce a reaction against the Crooked Cross. Is it too much to hope that, when that day comes, those who have been faithful to the Cross of Christ and suffered so much, will have a message that may gradually receive a wider hearing from a disillusioned people, nauseated by a propaganda that has wrought so much injury to their bodies and their souls?

The New Paganism

The epic story, here too slightly sketched, suggests certain reflections on the place of religion in human society. The new paganism invented by Hitler and his associates, like the Bolshevism of Stalin, demonstrates at once the necessity for a mystical element in political movements, and the grave dangers that are attached to it. The worship of the Messianic Führer, the belief in the racial election of the Germans, the laudation of force as an instrument of the Divine action, are all parts of the technique for attaining and retaining power. This religion must be swept away if the concentration of power inevitable in modern society is to be made fruitful for, and not destructive of, human happiness. But this can only be done, if the false mysticism be replaced by a true faith, by one that recognises the existence of a Supreme Moral Law of universal validity as the determining factor in the universe. To fall back on mere utility will fail once again to provide the necessary basis for human co-operation.

The Crooked Cross, in its perversity, has some light to throw on the meaning of freedom. It is not without significance that, when the Party, of which it is the symbol, triumphed over academic, industrial and political freedom, there remained one liberty that it could not subdue, the liberty to believe in that which is above all human systems.

In Volume III of the *Cambridge Modern History* that acute thinker, Neville Figgis, draws the following conclusions from his survey of political thought in the sixteenth century: "Religious liberty is rightly described as the parent of political." The idea of sovereignty is the first need for the true conception of the State. But it is no less necessary to realise its limitations. "Religious liberty arose, not because the sects believed in it, but out of their passionate determination not to be extinguished, either by political or religious persecution." When to-day the totalitarian State threatens more frightful tyrannies than any in the past, religious faith has an essential part to play in the maintenance of freedom.

NAZI AND NAZARENE

By

RONALD KNOX

NAZI AND NAZARENE

MOST of us, in youth, have greeted with impatient ridicule the argument that such and such a thing is the thin end of the wedge. Most of us, as part of the little wisdom we garner during life, are driven to the conclusion that there was something in it after all. And the short history of Nazi Germany might be represented by a surrealist picture consisting entirely of wedges; not, indeed, that the thin ends of them are very thin—the angle is often one of sixty degrees; but that has been the method of the Third Reich, and it has not failed yet. You see it in Hitler's rise to power, first figuring as the leader of a constitutional party, then allying himself with Hugenberg's Nationalists in order to secure a working majority, then playing the cuckoo in the Conservative nest. You see it in his foreign policy—his studious friendliness towards Poland until Poland's turn should come, and that was not until the swallowing of Austria had laid the flank of Czecho-Slovakia bare, and Czecho-Slovakia itself (in two gulps, this time) had been thoroughly assimilated. You see it, equally, in the Nazi encroachment on the Christian faith; above all in the Nazi encroachment on the privileges of the Catholic Church, which is the subject of this study.

The wedge-driving method has this obvious advantage —that you are continually playing off two human temperaments against each other. There is a temperament which is for resisting the first sign of aggression, yielding no inch to the suspected enemy, for fear he should take an ell; in a word, the temperament which is convinced that wedges have thin ends. There is another, more peaceful temperament which urges, "No, not yet; it would be an error to take our stand on such flimsy provocation as this; throw a sop to the wolves, in the hope that it may suffice them; wait until the situation becomes really intolerable before you strike." This latter temperament is for ever selling the pass, slope by slope, to the enemy. Where the foreign policy of the Reich was concerned, most of us have had illusions which time was destined to shatter; this is not the hour for recriminations. Just so, in his dealings with the Catholic Church, Hitler has continually taken advantage of those moderating counsels which have urged concessions in this crisis or that. He has played off the Innitzers against the Faulhabers.

Whether this kind of piecemeal aggression is due to a subtle, calculated policy, or whether the Third Reich is led on from one encroachment to another, as the vistas of possible self-aggrandizement open successively to its view, there is no need here to determine. Some represent Hitler as a chess-player of consummate skill, who has thought out all his moves a full decade ahead. Others regard him as an illuminist who acts upon the instinct of the moment, so that it is never possible to prophesy what he will do next—a view which has become especially popular with those whose duty it is to guess what he will do next. But in truth Hitler is not an ogre, he is a human being; and probably, like most of us, he lets forethought and opportunism wait upon each other; in shaping events, he allows events to shape him. I doubt if he has, personally, such bitter feelings towards the Catholic Church as many of those who have persecuted her; in the old days when he fought against Communism, I doubt if he realised that he would be concerned, one day, to combat her influence. But the logic of his own immoderate aims has driven him to it.

Before the Fuehrer

In fairness to both sides, something must be remembered which is customarily forgotten,[1] that the conflict between Nazism and the Church began before the Nazis came into power. In 1931, the Bavarian bishops issued a declaration which protested against the movement's racial doctrine, its attitude towards the Bible, and certain other aspects of its religious code. Priests were forbidden to take any part in it, and active members of it were to be denied the Sacraments. This did not prevent many Catholics from voting for the party at the crucial election; already the meet-them-half-way temperament had begun to assert itself; and, after all, anything was better than Communism. But friction between the official representatives of the Church and the official doctrines of the party had been, thus early, foreshadowed. It is also fair to remember that the Nazis, on their side, professed no love for the Church; there was no treachery, in this instance, about their approach. Nobody expected that the thin end of the wedge would be exactly a burglar's jemmy; but the householder had every reason to be on his guard, and not suffer his house to be broken up.

Germany went totalitarian in 1933. It was no matter for surprise that, in the course of that operation, the Centre party should have disappeared. All parties were merged in the Party, and the Centre, which for so many decades had

[1] See Michael Power, *Religion in the Reich*, pp. 12 *sqq.*

been the rallying-ground of moderate opinion, swinging to right or left as a pendulum was needed to redress the balance of the political machine, was the last kind of interference which would be welcomed by a Government pledged to desperate expedients. The gradual throttling of the Catholic Press, which was only completed in 1935,[1] might also have been expected; the totalitarian Government does not tolerate criticism, from whatever quarter, any more than it tolerates independent political action. So far, a grave wrong had been done, but it was a wrong done to democracy in general, not to the Catholic Church as such. All that had passed so far was only the preliminary to an assault.

It was understood, of course, to be the exact opposite. Before we condemn the compliance or the short-sightedness of those Catholics who helped, in spite of episcopal warnings, to vote Hitler into power, we must try to understand, as it is not easy for us to understand, the attitude of mind in which those who accept (without welcoming) a totalitarian Government strike the balance between their gains and their losses. The thing, it seems to them, has got to come; it is the only way in which the country can be pulled together, or it is the only way of avoiding bloodshed and constant friction; our political liberties must go; what remains to us? Our personal liberties, at least; a totalitarian *régime* can have no reason to grudge us those.

Political and Personal Liberty

It is to be remembered that political liberty and personal liberty are not the same thing; if you belong to a minority in a country where matters are decided by the

[1] See Edmond Vermeil, *Hitler et la Christianisme*, p. 61.

counting of heads, your personal liberty may be drastically curtailed. And this applies not only to the individual (as when a majority of your fellow-citizens determines to enforce prohibition laws), but to voluntary associations within the State, and above all to religious bodies. The Catholic Church, in particular, has had much to suffer from the democracies. Where she is in a minority, statesmen will often forbid her the liberty of teaching, or of public action, precisely for fear that the minority may grow into a majority, to the detriment of their own rival culture. In Germany, her position had been threatened by State Lutheranism on one side, by international Socialism on the other. Amid the tangle of political parties, German Catholics had been driven, unwillingly, to organize a political party of their own; it had seemed the only way of defending their personal liberty. When all the parties disappeared, the Centre with the rest, it looked as if personal liberty might be secured for the Church as the price of her political renunciation.

The new men who had come into power professed to be indifferent over the rival claims of Catholic and Reformed theology; international socialism was their professed enemy. Was it not reasonable to hope that Catholics would be left to live their own lives, undisturbed by the threat of State interference?

Nor was this merely an *a priori* expectation; there was an obvious parallel to be drawn from the situation in Italy. Events have moved so rapidly that it is difficult to carry our minds back to the state of things which existed less than ten years ago, when all Europe saw in Hitler a mere imitator of Mussolini. Mussolini, like Hitler, was a Catholic who had given up, so far as was known, the practice of his religion; there was no reason to think that he loved the Church. But, from the moment when the Partito Popolare was dissolved, he seemed clearly anxious to delimit the spheres of God and Caesar with accuracy, and abide by the delimitation. Why should not Hitler do the same? Catholic sentiment, in Germany as in Italy, was a useful bulwark against Communism; it was expedient for him, surely, to keep on the right side of it, even if it were true that a few extremists in the Nazi Party were trying to float a religion of their own.

The Concordat

This, at least, seems to have been the feeling in Rome, whatever misgivings German Catholics themselves may have entertained. The result was the Concordat signed in July, 1933, between the Holy See and the new government of the Reich. It was a diplomatic triumph for Hitler;[1] and was interpreted in the world at large as expressing a measure of agreement between the secular and the civil authorities which never in fact existed. Popular ignorance imagines that a Concordat is only drawn up where a country is on especially friendly terms with Rome. This is the precise opposite of the fact; a country which was on ideally good terms with Rome would not need to have a Concordat at all; and the existence of such a document implies that the two signatory parties are, in a more or less degree, distrustful of each other's intentions. It is an attempt to regularize a difficult situation by tying down either party, on paper, to a minimum of good behaviour. In July, 1933, the situation was not that Pope Pius XI believed Hitler

---

[1] "By the signature of the Concordat, National Socialism has been recognized by the Catholic Church in the most solemn manner possible."—*Völkischer Beobachter*, July 24, 1933.

would treat the Church well; he may have hoped that it would be so, and that a document formally attested would have some effect on Hitler's policy; but if there had been no distrust, there would have been no Concordat. Nothing could be more absurd than to represent the transaction as if it were meant that the New Germany and the Vatican were working hand in glove.

Two clauses in the agreement safeguarded the interests of Caesar. Each Bishop on his appointment was to take an oath of loyalty to the German State; and the Holy See undertook that the clergy should not belong to, or further the objects of, any political party. In return for this, the German Government promised, with almost suspicious alacrity, complete freedom to the Catholic schools, and to associations of Catholics for purposes other than political; meanwhile associations which were sponsored by the State should not interfere with the religious life, or form the religious conscience, of Catholic children and young people. In a word, the Church would never have to regret her action in allowing the Centre Party to be liquidated; the prvileges for which that party was prepared to fight should be hers without the necessity of fighting.

Six Days Later . . .

"Six days after the signing of the Concordat, the State duly promulgated the Sterilization Law, which gave powers for sterilization, by force, even of the blind." [1] Suddenness is a recognized part of the Nazi technique; the moving of a piece on some quite different part of the board, to make your opponent wonder how this move is connected with the one before, or whether it is connected at all. In

[1] Power, *op. cit.*, p. 34.

this case, it can hardly have been an accident that the new rulers of the Reich proceeded so quickly from an instrument of peace with the Catholic authorities to a legislative act so repulsive to Catholic principles.

There is no need to consider here the ethical implications of the measure. We are concerned with it, not as an act of persecution, but as an act of provocation. This, surely, was its immediate purpose. It was the thick end of the wedge, this time, thrust in to open the door for that crusade of race and force which has been the chief characteristic of the Nazi philosophy. Catholics were to realize, without loss of time, that the *régime* which had gained respectability by the signing of the Concordat intended to flout the convictions, not only of all Catholics, but of all Christians in Europe. It was clear provocation; why was it important that the provocation should come so soon?

For this reason above all—that the rulers of Germany wanted to make it appear, from the first, as if the Concordat had been broken on the Catholic side. A few pulpit declamations against the new law—and who could doubt that they would be forthcoming?—would lend colour to the claim that the bishops were not observing their pledge to support the Reich; after that, it would be possible to drive a coach and four through the Concordat and still maintain that you were not the aggressor. The Nazi technique never neglects propaganda. Very little colour may be needed to justify its actions before a public which only knows what it is allowed to hear, and is not encouraged to comment even on that. But always *some* colour must be found to excuse even its most flagrant performances. And whenever Nazi propaganda is taxed with persecution of the Church, its reply is always the same—that the Catholics began by refusing to keep "politics" out of the pulpit.

Actually, it was not till Cardinal Faulhaber preached his Advent course at the end of this same year, 1933, that a kind of official challenge was thrown down by the Church to the Nazi philosophy. But it was soon enough.

The year 1934 saw only the beginnings of that forward drive by which the Nazi culture, with Rosenberg at its head, aimed at filching from the Church the loyalty of youth. The reason for this was plain; at the end of that year a plebiscite was to be held in the Saar district, which would decide for or against its reincorporation in the Reich. Catholic influence in the Saar was strong; it would not do to let the Nazi State appear as the open enemy of the Church. As the youth organizations of Catholic Germany began to disappear, Hitler "received Cardinal Schulte and gave him verbally his promise that the rights of Catholics would be protected, and no article of the Concordat infringed." [1] Unconvinced, the bishops wrote a joint pastoral at their yearly meeting at Fulda, expressing their anxiety over the turn things were taking. It was confiscated by the Gestapo, and the faithful never saw or heard it.

The Oath of Loyalty

In a sense, the Concordat between the Reich and the Holy See was based on a fundamental misunderstanding. Pope Pius, in agreeing that the bishops should take an oath of loyalty to the German State, obviously did not intend anything more than a recognition of the German Government as the constituted government of the country. Catholic bishops might swear loyalty to it in the same sense in which Anglican bishops swear loyalty to his Majesty the King; without thereby binding themselves to accept, with-

[1] Power, *op. cit.*, p. 49.

out protest, every step which the Government might, from time to time, choose to take. They agreed, further, that they would not attempt to resuscitate the Centre party, in a country where parties had ceased to exist; that they would restrain their clergy from indulging in party activities. Was this to preclude bishops and clergy alike from protesting, even in sermons, against a pagan philosophy which the State was encouraging, against scurrilous attacks on religion in the party newspapers, against invasions of the Church's own rights, now apparently guaranteed to her? No reasonable political theory would admit such a conclusion. But the Nazi doctrine of the State construes all criticism of the Government and its measures as *lèse majesté;* you must accept everything in silence, or you are accused at once of political activity. Thus it may be said that the two signatories of the Concordat were not using terms in the same sense.

But, if so, the blame lies unquestionably at the door of the German rulers. They knew that they were coining a new language. Bishops and priests were to honour the constitutional government, and avoid acts which might endanger the welfare of the State—supposing that the French bishops had made a similar undertaking, would anyone in his senses have interpreted it as meaning a reverential silence in the face of any decree which the French Chamber might enact? You must not attach new senses to words, and then employ those words in drawing up a contract with a second party who does not share your vocabulary. Nor can Hitler have imagined for a moment that Pope Pius was signing the formula in that sense. No religious body could conceivably sign away, on a blank cheque, all its rights of criticism and of protest. The sixteenth and thirty-second clauses of the Concordat were face-saving clauses, to be used if and when it should become necessary to declare that the Concordat was a dead letter.

Next the Schools

The Saar plebiscite was taken at the beginning of 1935, with an intoxicating success for the cause of greater Germany. Once more shock-tactics were applied; fifteen days later "the official Bavarian press opened fire on the Confessional schools".[1] If a propaganda of mixed cajolery and intimidation could produce such results in a district which was only German by anticipation, what might it not do in a province which was already part of Germany? Goebbels brought all his batteries to bear on the public mind. "He who sends his child to the denominational school wrongs his child, and interferes with the unity of the people. We do not want Catholic or Evangelical schools, we want the school of Adolf Hitler." Such were the slogans which were posted up everywhere, and an intensive Press campaign followed up the posters. The effect was that in this year only sixty-five per cent of the Bavarian electorate voted in favour of the confessional schools, against eighty-nine per cent in 1933.

So far the success of the agitation, however lamentable, was not wholly unexpected. There will always be weaker brethren among the Catholic population, even of a traditionally Catholic country. There will be those who complain that the priests are too anxious to keep everything in their own hands; after all, it is possible to bring up your children as Catholics without sending them to exclusively Catholic schools. Hours were set apart for religious teaching in the provided schools (as we should call them), and

[1] Power, *op. cit.*, p. 50.

priests had the right of entry. Was it not doing the fair thing by one's children to give them the opportunities of advancement which were opened to them by being educated on the State model? Already it was clear that you had to be a good Nazi to get anywhere; it was not yet clear that it was impossible to be a good Catholic and a good Nazi at the same time; Rosenberg's eccentricities were not the established religion of Germany. Sixty-five per cent is as much as the Church can ordinarily count upon in the way of out-and-out supporters, where there is a conflict between the voice of ecclesiastical and civil authorities. If the thing had stopped there, the Church might legitimately have complained that the State had grossly exceeded its powers, by adopting a violently partisan policy in an issue where it should have remained neutral; that pressure had been exerted in defiance of the spirit in which the Concordat had been signed; but it would have had to be admitted that the human weakness of the weaker brethren had been to blame in selling the pass to the enemy.

But the thing did not stop there. A fresh vote was taken in 1936, after more propaganda, and the number of parents who voted for the confessional schools had been reduced to thirty-five per cent; another in 1937, and now the faithful remnant was reduced to four per cent. This speeding up of the tempo was frankly inartistic; an offence, not merely against justice, but against the law of averages. You cannot, by legitimate means, break down the resistance of a people so rapidly as that. A statistical triumph of this kind only serves to raise the suspicion that there has been manipulation of the votes. If there has not been manipulation of the votes, there must have been intimidation on a reckless scale to account for such a turnover. What is quite certain is that you have not taken a free vote.

Bullied into Submission

It is not relevant here to consider whether the Catholics in Bavaria and in other parts of the Reich (for these others fared no better) might not have shown a stronger front to the oppressor, and let their schools go down fighting, instead of being jockeyed into a show of acquiescence. Persecution is none the less persecution when it is successful. What chiefly unnerved resistance was probably the feeling that resistance would necessarily be in vain. It was quite clear, from the way in which education was being handled, that the Government was determined to get rid of the denominational schools, and many may have felt that it was better to let them have their way, for fear that they should make all Catholic education, even in the provided schools, impossible. What is quite certain is that the Nazis, by the constant threats to personal liberty which the Gestapo and the rubber truncheon secure, tyrannized over the consciences of the German Catholics, bullied them into submission without persuading them; and it is there that the essence of persecution lies. Indeed, it would have been more honest if the State had simply taken over the schools by open confiscation, instead of trying to persuade the world that their abandonment had been voluntary. Probably it is impossible for anyone who has breathed the air of a free country to realize the numbing effect which the new form of persecution has on those who are subjected to it: the shrieking of the Press, the fear of spying, of mock justice, of the concentration camp; above all, the impossibility of free discussion and open exchange of ideas. We have to remember, besides, that the wedge method always makes compliance with the Government demands something less than a sacrifice of absolute principle; religion was taught, and is still taught, in the State schools where the parents demand it.

It need hardly be said, that any argument for compliance which was based on the existence of "facilities" in the State schools was ill-founded. The wedge system was still at work; having, by 1937, obliterated the confessional schools, the Government proceeded, in 1938, to issue further legislation which was designed to take the sting out of all religious teaching everywhere. Lay teachers were allowed to do the work hitherto reserved for priests; priests were no longer to teach unless they could "guarantee that nothing in their religious classes would contradict the world-view of National-Socialism", and so on.[1] But indeed, no amount of facilities could suffice to counteract the Nazi atmosphere, the Nazi teaching. It is not as if you could go to school with the Nazis and acquire mere knowledge of facts, mere principles of taste and of criticism, such as a secular education would impart. The aim of the Nazis has been, from the first, to capture the imagination and the loyalties of youth; and to capture these for a perverted, though carefully elaborated, world-view. There is no room in the same child's head for the principles of Christianity, however languidly acquired, and for the racial ideology which has Hitler as its rule of faith, and the world-domination of the German race as its end.

The Hitler Youth

So much for the guarantee given by the Concordat that the Catholic schools should be allowed to continue. Too scrupulous to abolish them, the German Government had

[1] Power, *op. cit.*, p. 54.

forced the Catholic public to declare them unnecessary. But it is not only during school hours that the totalitarian State employs the time, and forms the character, of the young: it will manage their leisure for them. Here is a piteous reflection for anybody who has lived out half a century in this crooked world. There was an officer in the Boer War who distinguished himself by successfully defending an outpost of British resistance, which caught the public attention and the public fancy. His gallant services won him a well-merited reputation among his fellow-countrymen, and he determined to make good use of it. As Lord Baden-Powell, he organized and still directs the vast Boy Scout movement which counts its adherents in every corner of the earth. His calculation was that by the use of a little drill, a little uniform, and a great deal of comradeship, group discipline, and outdoor adventure, you could help in bringing up a generation of good citizens, of kindly and courageous men and women, perhaps even of loyal Christians. People might make fun of the methods by which the movement sought to capture the imagination of boyhood, totem-symbols and catchwords and all the rest of it, but nobody could quarrel with its aims, which were wholly patriotic and humanitarian, unless he were short-sighted enough to imagine that the need for patriotism could vanish overnight. England, once more, had shown an example to the world.

Corruptio optimi pessima; the example proved to be a fatal one. The peaceful thunders of Olympus have been stolen by the Titans; the model on which, it seemed, international brotherhood and universal good will were to dawn upon the world has been the model on which the new totalitarian States have built up the foundations of a contemptuous and unscrupulous nationalism. . . . It is a poignant reflection that Lord Baden-Powell, not many years since, was refused permission to land in Denmark because, as Chief Scout, he was wearing "uniform". In so far as it was his object to build up a healthy, resourceful, outdoors generation of boys, totalitarianism has faithfully imitated his ambitions. In so far as his design was to build up a generation which should fearlessly speak the truth, should help the weak, should show kindness to all its fellow-men, totalitarianism has borrowed his methods and warped them to the service of ideals miserably other than his own. To catch the boy out of school hours, to captivate his fancy with heroic legend, to discipline his outlook by catchwords and by community song—all that has been borrowed by the Nazis to build up a race pagan in morals, obedient to the hive-instinct of the new Germany, ferociously intolerant of all other cultures, worshipping nothing except brute strength.

Can the fountain of youth be so poisoned at its source? Will the dragooning of young Germans into Nazi ideals be a success, or will it breed, as intensive education sometimes does breed, a reaction? It is too early yet to say; the Nazi experiment is comparatively young; perhaps there will be a reversal in human fortunes which will leave historians permanently wondering whether the scheme would have worked. Meanwhile, it is certain that the institution of the Hitler youth, and the desire to make it the only youth-movement in the Reich, led to inevitable conflict between Nazism and the Church. In a sense, it may be said that German Catholicism invited attack by the very excellence of its organization. It had founded a political party—that party must go. It had an admirable network of schools, religious and secular—those schools must be denuded of their pupils. It was rich in youth movements, some of them affiliated with the boy scouts, some of them local and national—those movements must be engulfed in the single, all-assimilating corporation of the Hitler-youth.

The Concordat Defied

Once more, the Concordat had to be defied. By Article 31, it was laid down that, "Such Catholic organizations and associations as serve a purely religious, cultural, or charitable purpose, and as such are subject to the Church authorities, will be protected in their establishments and activities." [1] Religious associations may be of three kinds. Some of them will be frankly political in their aims and methods, like the Centre or the Partito Popolare. Some will confine their activities to the sacristy: pious sodalities which meet for prayer and mutual edification. Between these two extremes you have a no-man's land of promiscuous organizations which are covered, roughly, by the definition "cultural and charitable". The Nazi Government, it hardly needs to be said, lost no time in annexing the no-man's land. Either they would stretch the law so as to include these organizations under the term "political"; or they would simply merge them, in the name of efficiency, with non-religious organizations of their own. And, above all, the youth movements.

Baldur von Schirach, the head of the Hitler-youth, declared war against the Catholic organizations as early as March, 1934, when he told his audiences at Essen that "sport had nothing to do with religious beliefs", and the Catholic Jugendverbände were gravely mistaken if they thought they could retain "their political power" in a country which now had only one political orientation. [2]

[1] Power, *op. cit.*, p. 31.
[2] Vermeil, *op. cit.*, p. 67.

They held out bravely as long as it was possible to hold out. Two thousand German boy scouts went to Rome for the Holy Year in 1935. "On their return . . . they were set upon at Constance by the secret police. Their cameras, rucksacks, rosaries, musical instruments, souvenirs of Rome —everything they had with them was confiscated. Their shirts were torn off their backs. They did not see their belongings again." [1] The struggle could not be maintained; the strength of an association is its weakness—by a single decree, you can disband it or merge it in some parallel but wholly dissimilar organisation. In 1938, practically all the Catholic Jugendverbände were dissolved, and now the Hitler-youth is a necessary element in the training of every German. From this, it need hardly be said, every religious influence is jealously excluded.

"Enemies of the State"

It must not be supposed that this campaign for the destruction of religion was carried out with no other grounds to recommend it than the *Sic volo, sic jubeo* of the new Government. The Nazi technique always employs publicity (an art which it has studied intensively) to aid its onslaughts, just as it employs parachute troops to undermine the enemy's defences in military attack. Somehow the Catholics must be made to look as if they were the enemies of the State. Nothing would secure this more effectively than a series of legal condemnations; a legal condemnation, even in a country which has witnessed the Alice-in-Wonderland procedure of the Reichstag trial, carries with it a flavour of impartiality. And here the Nazis were in luck; it was not necessary for them to invent a law which

[1] Power, *op. cit.*, p. 58.

Catholics would be certain to break, since the exigencies
of their position called, quite legitimately, for currency
regulations which Catholics did break.

Early in the *régime,* in order to secure the stability of
the currency, a veto was imposed on the export of German
money to foreign countries. Special exemption was granted
to business firms which owed money abroad, none to individuals or to charitable organisations. Now, when the
mark fell, under the Weimar Government, many religious
orders had borrowed money from their foreign houses.[1]
They had no exports with which to repay these loans; they
could only repay them in money by smuggling. Conscience
thus presented them with rival claims; but, whereas the
repayment of the loans was a moral duty, the law forbidding the export of money was only a penal law, and could
therefore be infringed if you did so at your own risk, and
were prepared to face the consequences. From the point of
view of Catholic propaganda, it would have been very
much better if the debtors had defaulted, pleading the
impossibility of carrying out their contract. But it is not
surprising that they should have preferred the honest to
the legal solution. That they should be punished was not
unreasonable; that they should be savagely punished, was
not unexpected. The malice which lay behind these prosecutions showed itself in a more subtle way; it has been
pointed out [2] that the Nazi authorities deliberately spread
these trials over a period of months, taking them roughly
at the rate of one a week, so as to keep them continually
before the public eye, and give the impression that "the
Catholic Orders had no other occupation than the smuggling of German currency."

[1] Vermeil, *op, cit.,* p. 74.
[2] Power, *op. cit.,* p. 66.

Charges of Immorality

It seems to be generally admitted, however, that the staging of these prosecutions was not very effective in discrediting the Church. Early in 1937, a fresh attempt was made; this time the appeal was made to that large class of newspaper readers which delights in filthy revelations, and the character of the charges brought was such as to harden public opinion against the Catholic cause in the Schools question, which was then at its height. Some Franciscan lay-brothers, who had charge of mentally deficient children, were accused and found guilty of unnatural offences against those who were under their care. What truth there may have been in the allegations will perhaps never be known. There are black sheep here and there, no doubt, in the fold of St. Francis no less than elsewhere, and some of the accused may have been guilty. But it is to be remembered that the judges, officials in a Nazi country, were predisposed to credulity; it is to be remembered that the witnesses were, in the nature of the case, half-witted (one thinks of Van der Lubbe and his rôle in the Reichstag trial); it is to be remembered that abnormally constituted persons are notoriously subject to hallucinations in the matter of sex. In the case immediately under consideration, most of us will be content to suspend judgment.

But the handling of the affair by the authorities has, perhaps, no parallel in history. The whole of the controlled Press fed its pornographically-minded readers with revolting details, blazoned in its headlines, and promised them that this was only the beginning of a series of prosecutions, which would find no less than a thousand priests and nuns guilty of immoral conduct. In pursuance of this object, a great hunt was made for clerical delinquents in a society honey-combed with informers. Offenders who had already been found guilty and punished by ecclesiastical superiors were dragged to light. The effect was to show that a mountain had been made out of a molehill. The prosecutors succeeded in obtaining convictions against fifty-eight priests, out of a total of 25,000 priests in the Reich, and no nuns at all. The public must have realised, in spite of the gagging of the Catholic Press, that the whole business was a fiasco. Yet everyone who knows how mud sticks, how minds are impressed by insinuation rather than by proved fact, will be able to form some idea of the discredit brought upon the Church by this organised campaign of vilification.[1]

It is maintained by the Nazis, and by those who seek to excuse their conduct, that they have no quarrel with the Church as such—have they not left Catholics freedom of worship? Do not their places of worship remain open, and crowded?—but only with the Church's attempt to stake out a claim on the loyalties and enthusiasms of youth. Youth belongs to the nation, must be formed on a national model; it was necessary, therefore, to loosen the Church's hold on the nation's children, whether in school hours or out of it. That done, the Government of the Reich has no further quarrel with the priests; let them say Mass and conduct prayers and mind their own business. It would be difficult, in any case, to accept this account of the matter. We should be disposed to ask why the Press and the minor leaders of the party have conducted a campaign of abuse against Catholicism for the last seven years; why it has been necessary to send more than five thousand priests to prison. Can we really be sure that we have seen the worst

[1] Power, *op. cit.*, p. 71.

of State interference, that there is no more to come? In Germany itself, doubtless it was better not to risk a frontal attack; Catholicism numbers its millions. But if we want to understand the real Nazi attitude towards religion, we may be pardoned for devoting some attention to the treatment given to Catholics in other countries, which have come under the Reich's domination unwillingly.

Naked Persecution

When Austria came into the orbit of the German Reich, she was treated almost as a conquered country. The Catholic schools were all closed down without the formality of a vote, without any barrage of propaganda. Religious instruction remains in the State school where parents demand it, but it is mostly given by teachers fully imbued with Nazi ideals. What has befallen the German Catholics over a course of years befell the Austrian Catholics overnight. Still, they are allowed freedom of worship, like their co-religionists in Germany; they have not yet found themselves members of a proscribed fraternity.

In Poland it is otherwise; there, naked persecution has reigned ever since the conquest. That priests have been butchered everywhere in the course of mass executions does not perhaps belong to the story of persecution proper; the reason there is a war of cultures rather than of religions. It has been the German policy to choose as victims, when victims must be chosen, the intellectual and cultural leaders of Poland; that many of these should be priests is only to be expected. I am not suggesting that this is an extenuating circumstance; I am only pointing out that it does not necessarily imply hostility to the Catholic religion as such, or to the Christian religion as such. If Poland had been a Mohammedan country, it may be surmised that the officials of religion would have suffered equally.

What is more significant for our present purpose, because it seems to be an index of the general Nazi attitude towards Catholicism, is the wholesale closing of churches, the wholesale imprisonment or expulsion of the clergy. That is difficult to explain on merely cultural grounds. It is true that in Poland, as in Ireland, religion and patriotism are close bed-fellows. And you might have expected that the clergy in a conquered Poland would be subjected to irritating restrictions; that they would be watched by the police, that their sermons would be reported, the bishops' pastorals censored or suppressed; Polish Catholicism might reasonably be feared as a rallying-point for Polish national sentiment. But that does not account for what has happened.

"The Catholic churches in Poland were closed as from the beginning of November. The faithful of Poznan can attend Mass only on Sunday. . . . The administration of the diocese of Chelmo, embracing the whole of Pomerania, though not dissolved, is not allowed to function. The same applies to the administration of the diocese of Silesia, in Katowice, and that of the diocese of Kujawy, in Wlocavek. . . . The majority of the clergy of the above-mentioned dioceses are either in prison or interned in their own houses. In Poznan alone, over a hundred priests are imprisoned. . . . In the diocese of Chelmo alone, six hundred priests have been either imprisoned or interned in concentration camps." [1] "All the priests from the parishes of the Gniewkow deanery (sixteen in all), of the Lobzenica deanery (twelve), of the Naklo deanery (sixteen), and of the Znin deanery (twenty-one) were expelled. . . . Of the 261

[1] "German Atrocities in Poland" (Free Europe pamphlet), p. 34.

parishes in the Gniezno archdiocese, more than half have been deprived of their shepherds."[1] Dull statistics like these, which have little atrocity-value, are perhaps the surest index of German intentions in Poland; religion is to be starved out. And this, not because the conquerors of Poland could serve any useful end by turning the Poles into a virile nation; who in Germany wants to do that? The conclusion is irresistible that Nazi Germany, where it is not controlled by consideration of prudence, is bent on the destruction of Christianity as such.

Two Types of Persecution

It is our duty, always, to make some attempt at understanding those who disagree with us. And those who persecute the Church do so, commonly, not because they hate her in herself but because they identify her, obstinately, with something other which they hate. Two types of persecution may be easily distinguished by the colour they take from their historical context. There is persecution in the name of national security; where the rulers of a State, commonly of an aristocratic State, identify, or profess to identify, the Church with a foreign culture, suspect it, or profess to suspect it, of anti-national, because of its international, sympathies. The clergy, however strong and manifest be their patriotism, are regarded as foreigners because they are in relations with their co-religionists abroad, because some of them have been educated abroad; they cannot be hundred-per-cent citizens of their own country. So it was in old days when Catholics were persecuted in England: so it was in Germany at the time of the *Kulturkampf*. And there is persecution in the name of popular liberty; where

[1] English Catholic Newsletter, No. 15.

the partizans of a democratic revolution, in their eagerness
to sweep away all the landmarks of the bad past, profess to
find in the Church, and especially in her hierarchy, a relic
of the older order which must be swept away with the rest;
of course the clergy are the enemies of revolution, or how
was it that all went well with them in the days before the
revolution? So once more, though on quite different
grounds, the Church is persecuted.

The Nazi movement has, perhaps, both reasons for quar-
relling with Catholic influence in the Reich. For, on the
one hand, the German Catholics are bound by strong ties
to Catholics in other parts of the world, and the Nazi State
distrusts all such outside affiliations. And on the other
hand, Hitler's revolution, although we used to think of it
as a conservative revolution because it was anti-Communist
has proved, in fact, a break with the past hardly less radical
than Lenin's. Whether because they remind him that there
are cultures other than the German culture, or because
they remind him that there was a pre-Nazi Germany, Hitler might be expected to view the Catholics of the Reich
with distrust, and perhaps to harass them.

But does either motive account for the vigour, the pur-
posefulness, of the anti-Catholic drive? The Catholics of
Bavaria, and perhaps of the Rhineland, might be suspected
of sympathy with the old order of things; but not those of
Prussia and of the other German States. There, you feel,
the Lutherans might have been persecuted (as we know
they have been persecuted), and the Catholics let alone;
yet the suppression of Catholic influence has been nation-
wide. Nor, when you come to look into it, was there
much in the cry of "Foreign influence!" The German
Catholics had no love for France; they remembered the
anti-clerical laws, and they blamed France for the ill-success

of Brüning's Chancellorship. Russia they hated, like the Nazis; Italy, Germany's new friend, was endeared to them by the aid which it leant to the anti-Communist rising of General Franco. There was no reason in the nature of things why the new German Government should not have pulled well with the Church at first, if there had not been some more intimate ground of disagreement.

A War on Christianity

The fact is, unless all the symptoms of the struggle have wholly misled us, that for once the Church is being persecuted not because she is Catholic but because she is Christian. Wherever else we point to anti-clerical legislation, and denounce it, our non-Catholic friends are not slow to retort that the Church has invited attack by being untrue to the spirit of her Master. But not in Germany; there it is precisely because she is true to the spirit of her Master that she is held up to scorn. She has loved righteousness and hated iniquity; therefore she is in exile. Many of the Church's persecutors would have been moved to compunction, or at least to indignant disavowal, if they had had St. Paul's experience; if it had been said to them in a vision, "I am Jesus, whom thou persecutest". To a German statesman, it would be no news.

It is as if the mantle of the centuries had slipped away, and Christendom were faced with the prospect of converting the world afresh. May we be found worthy of the task; it is no light one.

WHEN I REMEMBER....

By

THE RT. HON. J. R. CLYNES, M.P.

Acknowledgement is due to Messrs. Hutchinson who have given permission for certain passages from Mr. J. R. Clynes' *My Life* to be reproduced here.

WHEN I REMEMBER . . . .

WHEN I look back, as through a telescope, down the vista of the years since I was a small boy running barefoot over dangerous oily floors, keeping pace with spinning machinery in an Oldham cotton mill, I realise with a shock that, since that time, England has been changed as though at the sweep of a wizard's wand.

But there was no wizard, just as there has been no Dictator. The almost incredible industrial reforms have been brought about instead largely by the courage, patience and sincerity of a band of self-educated visionaries in red ties and baggy trousers. I remember that particularly when I read Hitler's claims and promises and abuse. He has presented himself to the workers as the real Socialist who gets things done, and he never ceases to pour scorn on the old Social-Democratic Party, on what he calls "goody-goody meetings, where people talk about the brotherhood of the people". He has had the help of rubber truncheons, incendiarism and murder, and he has succeeded in sweeping away the whole trade union system, the whole machinery of collective bargaining. Trade union leaders have been shot or driven into exile; the workers' funds, their newspapers and printing presses have been confiscated; the Co-operative movement has been wiped out. Long hours, low wages and unlimited deductions from wages, Gestapo agents in every factory, workers moved here or there at the will of the dictator, this even in peacetime was the result of Hitler's revolution.

We have had a revolution, too, and I think it is time we spoke of it aloud for Dictators to hear. I have lived through it and been a part of it. When I was born in 1869 only a few visionaries talked of working men being admitted to Parliament. I have lived to see a foundry hand become Foreign Secretary, the son of a Keighley weaver created Chancellor of the Exchequer, and a miner Secretary for War.

The strange world into which I was born was dark and lurid; in the background stood the stately homes of England in all their peace and beauty; in the foreground were belching factories, slag-surrounded mines and grim mills, in which millions of bent-backed, ant-like figures ran to and fro, dutifully making the money by which the stately homes were financed, earning for themselves only coarse bread and the uncertain right to exist in squalor. In an inconspicuous corner where Oldham stands, amidst a great fever of mill work, surrounded by poverty and disease, malnutrition and ignorance, a small boy, sullenly eager to escape from the brutal slavery of school to the merciless thraldom of the mill, was very anxious to quiet the rumblings of an empty belly by contributing to the home exchequer the few shillings a week that a "little piecer" could earn. Myself!

A "Little Piecer"

I was a small, spindly, white-faced boy, and I had none of childhood's dreams. When I thought of anything beyond hunger, fatigue and the winter cold that pricked the very bones of my fingers and toes, my mind revolved with ambition around my next step in life. When I achieved the manly age of ten I could—if I were lucky—obtain half-time employment in one of the great cotton mills, whose chimneys darkened the sky.

At last my tenth birthday came, and I managed to obtain half-time work at the Dowry Mill as a "little piecer". My hours were from six in the morning each day to noon; then a brief time off for dinner; then on to school for the afternoons; I was to receive half-a-crown a week in return. As conditions were then I was counted lucky. But by that time my brother and sisters were becoming a serious drain on our combined resources. My father and I earned less than thirty shillings a week between us; and our total wages were not very much on which to pay rent, buy clothes and feed the family. Our food was bread, with butter when we could afford it, and lard or dripping when we could not; stews composed of vegetables and unwanted cuts of meat; peas and beans which filled us well and did not cost very much; and tea when we were lucky. Nothing else.

I worked at the spinning-frames, in my bare feet, since leather on those oil-soaked floors would have been treacherous. Often I fell, rolling instinctively and in terror from beneath the gliding jennies, well aware that horrible mutilation or death would result if the advancing monsters overtook and gripped me. Sometimes splinters as keen as daggers drove through my naked feet, leaving aching wounds. Running in and out, straining my eyes in the gaslit gloom to watch for broken threads, my ten-year-old legs soon felt like lead and my head spun faster than the machinery. As my aching fingers pieced up the broken ends of cotton I thought how lucky I was to have been born in a humane era when children could not be employed for more than ten working hours a day, and how much more dreadful must have been the conditions of child labour when my father was a boy. Heaven knows I was right!

At last the age of twelve came! I was free from the thraldom of school, where I had learnt nothing except a fear of birching and a hatred of formal education, and I was able to go forth a grown man into the world of work, able to earn ten shillings a week now, a full-time piecer. How often I had envied other lads a year or two older than myself—sunken-eyed waifs—who had already graduated into brave industry. At least they had finished with school; at least they were being paid real money each Saturday, and their parents left them a penny or two of it each week with which they could buy things really for themselves.

That was my childhood, and my prospects? I could dream daringly of surpassing my father's income some day, if I kept earnestly at my job, my father who earned twenty-four shillings a week as a labourer for the Oldham Corporation. And my scanty leisure—I remember no golden summers, no triumphs at games and sports, no bird-nesting, no tramps through dark woods or over shadow-racing hills. There was no wireless: no bicycles: newspapers only existed for educated people: there were no cheap books. I remember accumulating two weeks' pocket money to spend sixpence on a dog-eared dictionary and working through it in the evening after work from A to Zymotic. Candles cost me threepence or more each week. The dictionary was followed by an eightpenny copy of Cobbett's Grammar—but at that point I felt the need of some guide. An ex-schoolmaster held classes two nights a week, and when the fivepence I could contribute from the wages at the mill proved insufficient, I began to earn another threepence by reading the weekly newspaper to three blind old men in a stuffy, dusty Oldham cottage. Such, and the classes, was my secondary education.

And Now To-day

Now I want to take my eyes away from that "little piecer" and consider how to-day Britain brings up her children. She has a system which makes it possible to look after them before they are born and to continue looking after them until they are launched on the adventurous seas of active working-life, physically and mentally equipped to win happiness for themselves and carve out a useful citizenship for the State.

This is not easily secured, nor is it done without exception all over the country to the full extent. But it can be done and it is done. The opportunities are there. The powers are there. The key to their full use lies with the local authorities. The driving force behind those local authorities rests with the people themselves.

That is a point of extreme importance. The system of education and child welfare has probably no superior in the world. True, its administration to a large extent is permissive and not compulsory on the local authorities (apart from the basic education organisation itself) but the complete use of the whole system depends on the fathers and mothers of the children and on the influence they bring to bear in local administration. In that sense it is a wholly democratic and not a dictated affair.

Maternity Welfare

Let me sketch in broad outline what can and what does in many parts of the country happen to the British child. First there are ante-natal clinics. Wide powers are given to local authorities under the maternity and child welfare legislation for the supervising of nursing and expectant mothers and for looking after the welfare of children up to the age of five.

Admittedly there are not as many ante-natal clinics as there should be, but a wonderful work is done in those that have been established. We have realised in this country to what an extent a child's future may be determined before it is born, how much of the physical and mental quality of our coming citizens depends on how we deal with the expectant mother. So the expectant mother is able to go to the ante-natal clinic for advice and medical attention, and how much this has meant has been shown not only by statistics but in an easily observable increase in health and happiness.

Take infant mortality, i.e., deaths of children under one year per thousand births. Just before the Great War the rate for England and Wales was 108 per thousand. The last available official figures showed a reduction to 58 per thousand. It is still unfortunately true that, while this remarkable decline has taken place all over the country, there is an illuminating difference between the rates in poor and overcrowded districts and those in more prosperous and widely-spaced neighbourhoods.

But this is not always the case, and the exceptions show how much can be done where the least might be expected. Take Bermondsey, a London Borough where the people are mostly very poor and where there are many unemployed or casually employed. Within twelve years, Labour rule there nearly halved the infant death rate, and I remember Mary Sutherland, the Chief Woman Officer of the Labour Party, writing: "It is safer to be born in poverty-stricken Bermondsey to-day than in many well-to-do areas, thanks to the bold housing policy of the Council, and to the whole-hearted way in which the Maternity and Child Welfare Act has been carried out."

The attack has been made. We have shown the way. And the results are a great justification.

At the ante-natal clinics the expectant mothers can be provided with free milk.[1] If, after all this precautionary care, she takes the wise advice given there, the expectant mother will have her baby in a maternity hospital, where she and the infant will receive treatment equal to that purchased by the highest fees of those more fortunately placed. There is still a shortage of such hospital accommodation in a number of areas, but before the outbreak of war continual progress was being made, and that must and will be extended in happier days. Side by side with this, there is a system of home service, and last year more than 3,000 women health visitors in England alone paid between them nearly 8,000,000 visits.

So the baby is born, and the mother, tended and nourished, can continue to go to a clinic or a child welfare centre still obtaining advice, medical attention, milk, and in many cases, food.

The Nursery School

At the age of two there comes a change for the baby. In the enlightened areas there is a Nursery School—a bright, airy, well-designed place, run by specially qualified and understanding women. In other districts there are nursery classes in the elementary schools. Gently the toddler is led along, "picking up", rather than being "taught", invaluable things like personal hygiene and the budding ideas of

[1] Now under the Government's milk scheme all expectant and nursing mothers and children under 5 can obtain milk either free or at half price.

service and friendly help. Quickly they begin to take a pride in their individual washing materials (labelled with a picture of a bird, a flower or an animal), in their own toothbrushes (and in the necessity for using them), in helping to serve meals and to "clear up" as soon as they are able to do so.

They eat their hot dinner, go to rest in their cribs, get the first glimmerings of "education" and then they are taken home—there to teach their fathers and mothers and older sisters or brothers what they have learned. There are thousands of small households to which these little children have brought instruction. Regard the young child, if you like, as the human counterpart of the pebble tossed into the pool. The circle of the ripples widens and widens. So it is with the spreading communal and comradely influence of these Nursery School children.

In the best Nursery Schools the children have three meals a day. In some of them, children who come in with rickets are cured within eighteen months.

Here is another and a very vital problem—that of nutrition. It is not much good trying to teach an ill-nourished child. The maternity and child welfare legislation gives power to local authorities to provide food free or at cheap rates to necessitous mothers and young children. That this power is not used nearly to the extent that it should be is not the fault of our system, but is due to many local authorities lagging behind. I said in a recent article that by peaceful means we have secured reforms in working-class life beyond the dreams of our fathers. I added: "Much yet remains to be done and by means of a wholesome discontent more will be obtained."

A wholesome discontent. I would like to emphasise that. An orderly expressed discontent under our democratic method can reap the complete harvest. That is where the complete cutaway from dictatorship methods comes. What we have won, what we are going to win, are things not tossed to the people by dictators but things gained and cherished by the people because justice accompanies freedom.

Ante-natal treatment, child welfare centres, home service, the provision of food and milk, nursery schools, Maternity Hospitals—all these things are helping towards healthy babies and happy mothers, but there is room for advancement, and the Standing Joint Committee of Industrial Women's Organisations—which is the Labour Party's Advisory Committee on women's questions—pointed the way to a tremendously necessary national benefit when in a Labour Party pamphlet entitled *Children's Charter* it said: "It is, of course, important that the welfare centres should be used as fully and freely as possible by poor mothers, but it is equally important to emphasise that they provide a service which *all* children need and which can better be met collectively than by parents individually."

A Chance to Learn

Britain has now got the baby not only born but also, where there is a nursery school, or nursery classes (the country should be speckled by them), brought to the age of five—healthy, happy and with at all events some basis on which real education can be founded.

The primary school and the subsequent stages follow and every boy and girl is assured of full education for the nine years following the nursery school age of five. Those who by their natural gifts are able to take advantage of added opportunities can go farther. Free places with maintenance grants in secondary schools are increasing in number and should still further increase. For those who can fight through there are university opportunities.

In that remarkable book, *The Silent Social Revolution*,[1] the author shows how a people "with a very practical genius" has built up in a matter of forty years a public educational system "which, if progress continues at the same pace in the years to come, should soon be able to challenge comparison with that of any other country in the world."

He says: "A visitor to one of our elementary schools to-day will observe the economy and efficiency of its discipline, will note its atmosphere of orderliness and precision, and will carry away an indelible impression of the good manners and politeness with which all schools now seek to welcome their guests. Lest he should take these things for granted, it is as well that he should be reminded before he leaves that it is barely fifty years ago that the attendance officer who wished to penetrate one of those slums from which some of the children may still come had to take a police officer with him. It is well, too, that he should be reminded that the streets of London were swarming with waifs and strays who had never attended school, and who slept together in gangs in such places as the Adelphi Arches, on barges, on the steps of London Bridge, in empty boxes on barges—covered with tarpaulins or old sacks."

A Worthy Beginning

I would like to quote again from this valuable and revealing book a passage which seems to me singularly appropriate at the moment: "Nothing is more exasperating to those to whom social reform is religion in action than the

[1] G.A.N. Lowndes (Oxford University Press).

readiness with which the English neglect, forget or mini-
mise their achievements. The visitor from Central Europe
will tell with enthusiasm of the decline of illiteracy in his
country since the war. The Englishman scarcely knows the
meaning of the word, still less does he trouble to enquire
whether illiteracy still exists in England.

"It is in fact probably true to say that surprisingly few
Englishmen, even among those who are engaged in the
service of education, would feel equipped to give at short
notice a reasoned and convincing statement of the case for
public education. Again, although most people will readily
assent to the dictum that educational expenditure is long-
range expenditure, few are qualified to prove its truth by
showing what the long-range expenditure incurred by past
generations has achieved."

His conclusion is as follows: "In the creation of an educated democracy complacent satisfaction with the degree of
progress so far achieved can find no place. The millennium
is still a long way off. So long as there is one child who has
failed to obtain the precise educational treatment his individuality requires; so long as a single child goes hungry,
has nowhere to play, fails to receive the medical attention
he needs; so long as the nation fails to train and provide
scope for every atom of outstanding ability it can find; so
long as there are administrators or teachers who feel no
sense of mission, who cannot administer or who cannot
teach, the system will remain incomplete.

"But (the italics are mine) *when the social historian of
the future comes to write of the development of public
education in England in the first sixty years of its existence
as a compulsory force, he may feel that, considering how
much had to be accomplished, the task was worthily begun.*"

Those words I think we can all take to heart. They are

words which Dictators and their servants and sycophants can also take to heart.

The bare date outline of our education enactments during the last sixty-odd years is as follows: 1833, the first Government grant for education, which amounted to £20,000 for school buildings; 1880, compulsory education for children from five to eleven years; 1891, free education in all elementary schools and the age extended to twelve; 1906, the School Meals Act which gave permission to local authorities to feed necessitous children on attendance days; 1914, another School Meals Act which extended the scope of feeding to week-ends and holidays; 1918, an Education Act which gave power to set up Nursery Schools and Open-Air Schools; 1921, another Act relating to the same matters and giving local authorities further powers and the opportunity of receiving State grants for the purposes of these two types of school.

The last report of the Board of Education showed that local educational authorities in England and Wales spent about 96½ million pounds in 1937–8 which included £16 3s. 2d. per child for elementary education alone. It told how steady progress was being made with reorganisation of the elementary school system on the lines of the Hadow Report on the education of the adolescent. It told, too, how practically all authorities now make more or less complete provision in the medical services for treatment of defects covered by the regulations. The treatment of minor ailments, it was stated, dental treatment, and treatment for defective vision are undertaken by nearly all local educational authorities, while orthopædic treatment covers nearly ninety per cent. of the public elementary school population. All authorities provide clinics.

This is no occasion to discuss such matters as secondary

and still further advanced education, commercial and technical training schemes and the like.

Our educational development has reached a high mark, although there is admittedly much to be done. There is still more to be done in the matters of free feeding and general nutrition. Tremendous strides have been made in curative work. We need faster and greater strides in preventive work. Much has been done there during the last quarter of a century, but much remains.

The Rights of Children

The fundamental thing is that in this country the rights of the children have been recognised.

I will go back for a moment to *The Silent Social Revolution*. The author says: "Every pass-degree student of history knows that the Duke of Wellington exclaimed that the battle of Waterloo was won on the playing-fields of Eton; every honours student knows that he never said anything of the kind. He did, however, admit that it was 'a damn near thing'. Similarly the Great War may not have been won in the little asphalt yards of our public elementary schools, or even in the more spacious playgrounds of our local grammar and secondary schools, but it would have been a far nearer thing than Waterloo had not those schools been sending out year by year after 1902 hundreds of thousands of scholars a little better trained, a little more accustomed to leadership, than their prototypes of twenty years before."

In the future someone may point the same lesson in relation to the events through which we are passing to-day.

There are, of course, many other aspects of the successful fight that has been waged on behalf of the children. In my own childhood even toddlers could be employed and I was a child myself when a Workshop Act was passed prohibiting the employment of children under eight years but permitting half-time work for children of from eight to thirteen years.

In my manhood years street trading for all children was forbidden by law, and I was "getting on" when, in 1920, work for all children under fourteen was ruled out.

Much the same sort of progress has taken place in connection with juvenile delinquency. Enormous strides, including the probation system, have been made. More and more Labour men and women have got on the magisterial benches and on to committees concerned with the tribunals and institutions dealing with children.

The present approved schools and remand homes may not be ideal, but they do give delinquent children a greater chance than ever they had before and further progress is still being fought for and achieved.

Then there are such things as the Playing Fields Movement together with the efforts made by enlightened local authorities to provide playing fields for children instead of leaving them to scamper in the streets; there are the cleared slums and the open spaces which have taken their place—all making for the health and the fitness of a young generation who will know how to use the peace that will follow vanquished dictatorship. Their fathers are fighting for that peace. They themselves will be spiritually, mentally and physically prepared to safeguard it.

All this is what Britain has done, and is doing, for its women and children with the object of building up a healthy people fit to play their proper part in the work of the nation.

Those Bad Days

And now what does our country do for its citizens when they are grown-up and go out in the world? It is impossible to answer that question without feeling a glow of pride in our achievements. Looking back again on the changes I have seen in my own lifetime, I am amazed at the tremendous strides that have been made in providing greater comfort, happiness and security for the men and women of Britain. I am not complacent; I am not satisfied. There are many reforms yet to be made; much progress still to be registered, but it would be ungenerous and unreal not to recognise all that has been done.

When I was born, the social and economic conditions in this country were appalling. There was no Health Insurance; no Unemployment Insurance; no Workmen's Compensation. An accident at work would send the breadwinner home to bed and there would be no help for his family in its hour of need, except the wicked old Poor Law System, the Bumbledoms so graphically described by Charles Dickens. My own father in his late working life was disabled by an accident. But there was then no compensation. For a few weeks he received charity gifts from the employer. The experience made me an ardent advocate of compensation, and my first speech in the House of Commons thirty-four years ago was on this subject.

In those bad days prolonged sickness or unemployment meant that the family had to sell its household goods, to live in bare rooms, in hunger and in rags, and even to send little children out to work at seven or eight years of age to bring in something, at least, to keep the home going at all.

Even when I came of age the conditions were still appalling. London dockers were on an average getting somewhere in the neighbourhood of ten shillings a week, sweating was widespread, slums were festering sores in the State.

Starving Crowds

"Unemployment brought a terrible train of consequences," says R. H. Gretton, in *A Modern History of the English People*, 1880–1922, "in that it finally submerged workmen who could never recover from a fortnight's failure of work, and were thrust down into pauperism beyond remedy". There was still no provision for the unemployed; no State help for the sick; the Poor Law, feared and hated by the poor, and intermittent charitable efforts remained the only means of succouring men, women and children out of work or ill through no fault of their own.

As late as 1903, Mr. Justin McCarthy was writing: "The workhouses have no space left in which to pack the starving crowds who are craving every day and night at their doors for food and shelter. All the charitable institutions have exhausted their means in trying to raise supplies of food for the famishing residents of the garrets and cellars of London's lanes and alleys."

That year there were daily processions of unemployed in the streets of London carrying collecting boxes and singing, "The Starving Poor of Old England". That year Jack London, the famous American novelist, told the tragic story of the great queues outside London's casual wards, of the numbers turned away or compelled to walk the streets all night without home or food.

What We Have Done

I do not write this because of any ghoulish desire to look back over the past, but because I am afraid that many of our younger people, now enjoying the things for which we fought, do not sufficiently appreciate all that has been done to make this old country of ours a better and brighter Britain.

Let me tell them of some other things.

Unemployment

Take Unemployment. Altogether about 15¾ millions in Great Britain are now insured against being out of work. Over four-fifths of the workers in Great Britain earning £250 a year or less benefit by this scheme.

Thus, in the year ending March 31, 1936 when unemployment was declining, there were over 4 million claims for benefit—many of them for short periods, others for long periods. Under the general scheme (there is a special scheme for agricultural workers) benefit is paid for 26 weeks in any insurance year, but persons with exceptionally good insurance records can be granted benefits up to 52 weeks in an insurance year. At the outbreak of war the scales of benefit were: Adult 17s. (since raised to 20s.), wife 10s., child 3s. (since raised to 4s. for the first two children).

Some people have tried to throw discredit on this great social experiment by calling payments made under it "doles". But this is entirely unfair and improper. Unemployment insurance pay is a legal right for which the workman, together with his employer and the State, has paid in equal shares.

It is one of the privileges and rights of our free country

that men and women who cannot get work through no fault of their own shall have the opportunity to draw quite legally—and in a dignified way—the wherewithal to live.

In my younger days we used to fight for "Work or Maintenance". We have still, unhappily, many unemployed—we have not got for them the full maintenance we should like, but we are far away from those days when there was no provision at all for those without work.

But this is not all. When Statutory Unemployment Benefit is exhausted, there is the vast machinery of Unemployment Assistance which continues to operate and to provide further benefits as long as the recipients remain within the field of employment.

We have complaints to make against the administration of Unemployment Assistance; we have opposed the Means Test; we think that payments should be more generous, but none of us would deny that there have been tremendous improvements.

And beyond this there is still the machinery of Public Assistance to come to the aid of the residue of hard cases outside of Unemployment Assistance.

One thing is certain. No man or woman in this England of ours need starve. If a person is destitute, if there is not money coming in to provide the basic needs of life, it is the duty of the Authorities to come to his assistance in one form or the other. And this assistance is not alone concerned with money or food; it also embraces medical service to supply medicines and surgical aid to those in need. The old conception of the Poor Law is being broken down and in its place is being built up the conception of a broad, humane system of social service through which all our poorer neighbours will be treated as self-respecting citizens.

A Sense of Security

Just as we may tend to under-estimate the advantages of Unemployment Insurance and Public Assistance, so we may do the same with National Health Insurance.

Up to 1912 practically nothing had been done by the State to help the many men and women—young and old—suffering from ill-health, who had lost their wages and had not the necessary money for medical attention, medicines and surgical appliances. Many men and women have, in the past, left their homes too ill to work and come to early graves because they could not afford to take time off, or secure necessary medical attention. Many, for the same reasons, developed chronic sickness or incapacity.

I remember this country rocking with political controversy when State Health Insurance was introduced by Mr. Lloyd George. Society women organised a great campaign against "stamp-licking" and lots of people thought it scandalous that employers should help to pay towards a scheme of Health Insurance.

All that has died down. Everybody now realises the value of Health Insurance, even if it be far from perfect. But does everybody really appreciate what an integral part it is of the free institutions which we are called upon to defend? So many people take all these things for granted without thinking for a moment of what they would lose, of what we all should lose, if dictatorship triumphed.

Over 18,000,000 people in England and Wales and Scotland are covered by National Health Insurance. Over £33,-000,000 annually is paid out in sickness, disablement, medical and other benefits. Benefit not only covers sickness pay but also medical treatment, medicines and drugs and, varying in amount according to the approved society, optical,

dental, surgical aid and convalescence. There is also maternity benefit. Figures vary from year to year, but, in a normal
twelve months, Health Insurance benefit is paid to 8,000,000
people.

Workmen's Compensation covers roughly speaking anyone under a contract of service—that is virtually the whole
working population. For death due to a fatal accident at
work, compensation is paid in lump sums ranging from
£200 to £600. In the case of accidents, weekly payments
are made. The fight to establish for the British workman
the right to compensation for death and injury sustained at
work has been long and sustained. Even now there are
many anomalies which the Trade Unionists would like to
amend. But no one out of Bedlam would deny the progress
which has been made since the first Workmen's Compensation Act was introduced nearly fifty years ago.

Now there is at least some sense of security for all those
who are injured at work in the great industries of this
country—in cotton, wool, engineering, docks, mines, rail-
ways, shipping and other miscellaneous trades.

As the years go on, industrial diseases which add to the
toll of incapacity or death are embodied in the schedules.
The total liability of employers is estimated to be about
£12 to £13 million annually.

For the veterans of industry there are Old Age Pensions.
Over 3,000,000 people over the age of sixty-five at present
draw these pensions of 10s. per week, and under new Government proposals this is to be supplemented for about
275,000 pensioners who at present receive aid from Local
Authorities. In addition another 310,000 women between
60 and 65 are to receive pensions.

This question is still a matter of political controversy
and I shall not comment upon it here. We can argue as we

like as to whether the amount paid is large enough, but our conclusions will not upset the undeniable fact that much has been done to give greater comfort and support to the older people in their declining years. That I want to give them more does not in the least detract from what has already been done. And don't forget how, in some parts of the country, enlightened local authorities have provided housing and special amenities for the old folk and so greatly brightened their lives.

Housing

I could go on to tell how under successive Governments —of all parties—the housing conditions of the people have steadily improved. There are still slums, but they become fewer. There is still overcrowding, but it is decreasing.

In many of the great centres of population there has been amazing progress in the last few years. In the fresh air, away from the smoke of the cities, fine new estates have arisen, well-planned and soundly built. Roads have improved. Sanitation and other efficient municipal services have in most districts lifted up the standard of life of our people to a most significant extent.

To these improvements I gladly bear testimony. Compared with when I was a boy the condition of the young people is immeasurably better. They are better-fed, better-clothed, better-educated. When I was young, the whole of working-class life was drab, dull and depressing: to-day there is colour and variety that many of us older men never knew.

There is more opportunity for leisure; in the old days all work and no play made Jack a very dull boy. Hours of labour are shorter, conditions of employment better, wages higher. And much of this improved standard is due to the work of the Trade Union and Labour Movement which has banded men and women together in democratic organisations in order to make life more tolerable for all. But, of course, it is not the work of the Trade Union and Labour Movement only. To pioneers like Robert Owen and Lord Shaftesbury, to countless men and women of goodwill who have never identified themselves with any Party, to progressively minded people in all the political Parties, the workers and the nation owe an incalculable debt.

Only recently there has been a new drive for holidays with pay. There have been initial successes. There will be more. The day will come when every family in this country will have the opportunity to take a real holiday every year.

But if I could only convey to my younger readers the true extent of what has already been done, it would be worth while writing this pamphlet for that alone. It is indeed only in recent years that the great bulk of the population has been able to take any holidays at all. Now they are becoming a good habit. In the old days a hurried visit to the seaside for a few hours, or a charabanc outing, was all that a holiday meant.

Relate that significant change to other remarkable changes and it is possible to have some idea of what this new and developing social England means to all of us. And to the weaving of this fabric of our material life our magnificent social services have made a great contribution.

Any Young Couple

A young couple sets out in life. At every stage they come in contact with the advantages which come from living in this country with its advanced sense of public responsibility.

Their new house has most likely been built under a State or municipal housing scheme.

When the first baby is on its way, the mother will, in very many cases, receive advice and treatment at the local clinic. The child may first see light of day in a municipal maternity home, or be brought into the world by a municipal midwife.

The child welfare centre will keep a watchful eye on the new arrival; it will be weighed and examined; milk and special foods will be provided at reduced rates.

At five years, or often before, it will toddle off to a state school; it will be educated, medically examined, and later given the chance to go forward to advanced and higher education.

If the father is out of work or ill, he will claim for unemployment or health insurance; if he is hurt at work, he will make a claim for Workmen's Compensation.

If the couple live on to ripe old age, they will be able to claim from the State, something at least to keep the wolf from the door in their few remaining years.

All these services—costing the citizen and the community many millions a year—add enormously to social values in our country.

They are indeed an addition to real wages. Every improvement on these lines augments the social income and makes life easier and better for the vast mass of the common people.

Looking Back

My memory goes back again to the "little piecer" who was myself; to the boys and girls I knew, wakened at four or five o'clock in the morning, to work twelve or fourteen hours and then to stagger home half-asleep—only to be awakened once again in the early morning until life became one long torture.

I recall once more the earlier days of my Trade Union work when we were struggling to build up for the people of this country a decent standard of living with some sense of status and dignity.

When I remember all that has gone I find it impossible to understand those people who are unready in these days of national emergency to stand up for the privileges and rights we have won for ourselves.

German broadcasters in English may try to score debating points by calling attention to social injustices which we have criticised over and over again, but we can do that much better. They will not deceive the British workers who have far too much common sense to wish to abandon their solid advantages for the tyranny and misery of the Nazi State.

For myself, the path of duty is clear. This civilisation of ours—built on ordered freedom and reason—must be upheld by every just and right means. To surrender one inch to the claims of Hitlerism is to endanger everything—moral and social—which has been built up here. A victory for Hitlerism would mean the destruction of social services, of Trade Unionism, and of the standards of life we have established for our families.

A victory for Hitlerism would level our country down to the basis of a Slave state. I will have none of it and I am confident that my fellow-countrymen will resist with all their might and main this menace to their common welfare.

FOR CIVILIZATION

By

C. E. M. JOAD

FOR CIVILIZATION

I. The Special Excellences of Man

WHEREIN are to be found the distinctive characteristics of our species? In what, that is to say, do men differ from and excel the beasts? In swiftness or ferocity? The deer and the lion leave us far behind. In size and strength we must give way to the elephant and the whale; sheep are more gentle, nightingales more melodious, tortoises longer-lived, bees more co-operative, beavers more diligent. The ants run the totalitarian State much better than any Fascist. The truth is that our bodies are feeble and ill-adapted to survival; they are the prey of innumerable diseases; their enormous complexity means that they can go wrong in a vast number of different ways, while so poorly are they equipped against the vagaries of the climate, that it is only by clothing ourselves in the skins of other animals that we can survive. Hence to pride ourselves on any of the qualities I have mentioned, is to pride ourselves on qualities in respect of which the animals exceed us. Wherein, then, does our distinction, which is also, as we like to believe, our superiority, lie? The answer is, I suggest, that it lies in three things.

Reason: The first of these is our reason. Man, said Aristotle, is primarily a reasoning animal. He has, in other words, a mind which can reflect, discover causes, find reasons why, probe the secrets of nature, plan the future and meditate upon the purposes of life. Reasoning is broadly of two kinds. First, there is theoretical reasoning. Man is moved by curiosity and has a disinterested desire to *know* simply for knowledge's sake. The outcome of this desire is science, mathematics, philosophy, history, is in fact, the whole body of knowledge which constitutes our inheritance from the past and which moulds the mind of the present. Secondly, there is the reasoning which we perform in order to secure practical results. Applying the conclusions of theory to the practice of living, man has transformed his world, changing his environment more completely in the last hundred and fifty years than throughout the whole of the preceding two thousand.

Morals: Secondly, there are morals. Everything in nature except man acts as it does because it is its nature so to act. It is, therefore, pointless to argue whether it is *right* to act as it does; pointless to exhort it to act differently. We do not say of a stone that it ought to go uphill, or blame a tiger for tearing its prey. When, however, we consider a human being, we can say not only "this is what he is like", but also, "that is what he *ought* to be like." Man, in other words, and man alone, can be judged morally. What is the reason for this distinction between man and nature? It is to be found in the fact that man has a sense of right and wrong, so that, whatever he may in fact do, we recognise that he *ought* to do what is right and eschew what is wrong; we recognise also that whatever he may in fact do, he is *free* to do what is right and eschew what is wrong. Man is thus set apart from everything else in nature by virtue of the fact that he is a free moral agent. Many would attribute this unique moral nature of man to the fact that he possesses or is an immortal soul made in the image of his Creator. It is not, however, necessary to add this conclusion in order to recognise that, just as man has a reason in virtue of which he desires and achieves knowledge, so he has a moral faculty in virtue of which he desires the good and strives after what he takes to be right.

Sense of Beauty: Is there any other characteristic which is distinctive of the human species? It seems to me that there is, and that it is to be found in man's sense of beauty. Man recognises and responds to beauty in the natural world and creates for himself images of beauty in paint and sound and stone. As we owe to man's reason science and philosophy, and to his moral sense ethics and justice, so to his sense of beauty we owe art. It is not only in his ability to create beauty that man's distinctiveness lies. Not less important from the point of view of the community is the ability to recognise and respond to beauty in those of us who cannot create. The sense of beauty is allied to that of right and wrong; a good life has a certain beauty, just as intercourse with beauty in art and literature affects our attitude to life, making us more sensitive to and considerate of the feelings of others, more resentful of cruelty and injustice, more critical of vulgarity and superficiality. We should no doubt read for the pleasure of reading; yet it may well be asked if pleasure is all that we are entitled to expect from fine literature. If a book excites thought, if it stimulates the sense of beauty, the sense of pity or the sense of sympathy, if it helps in any way towards the understanding of our fellow creatures, if it increases our vitality, if it awakens our conscience and thus indirectly influences our personal conduct—if it accomplishes any of these things, then it has succeeded.

THE VARIOUS EXCELLENCES OF MAN

Let us suppose that I am right in regarding these three —reason, morals, and the sense of beauty—as the distinctive

attributes of man, and knowledge, goodness and beauty as
the goods or values which man alone can recognise, and let
us proceed to ask the question: "Wherein is man's highest
—development to be found?" Some men, it is obvious, are
more fully and representatively human than others; are,
that is to say, better or more typical specimens of what our
species is, when it is taken at its best. By what marks are
we to recognise them? Clearly we shall find them in those
who have developed to their fullest extent the distinctive
characteristics of humanity; not, that is to say, in the
strongest or the most ruthless or the most determined or
the most powerful or the wealthiest or even the bravest
members of our species, but in those in whom the characteristics of intelligence, goodness and good taste are
most highly developed.

This brings me to a new point. In order that men may
develop their distinctively human characteristics, their
—development must be free. If a growing thing is to attain
its full stature, if it is wholly to realise its nature, then, we
are all agreed, it must be allowed to grow in its own way.
It may require, indeed, it does require, to be trained, but
the training must develop, not distort. Cramp it, curtail it
and suppress it and though you may turn it into something different, though you may conceivably improve it, it
will no longer be its natural self. What is true of a living
organism, is true also of a human being; is true, therefore,
of the distinctive attributes of a human being. Freedom,
that is to say, is a necessary condition of their development.

1. FREEDOM AS A CONDITION OF KNOWLEDGE

First, as to the reason: it seems to me a good thing, good
that is to say, in itself, that the reason should work as it

pleases; that, in other words, I and everybody else should not only be allowed to come to the conclusions that seem right to us, but should be permitted to say what these conclusions are and why they seem right. I do not know how to prove that this is a good thing; I just see it to be so, just as I see kindliness to be a good thing and cruelty an evil one. But though I cannot prove, I can find supporting grounds for my belief.

In the first place, most of us are agreed that truth is a good thing; for the truth is something that we all want to know. Yet how is truth to be reached, unless men's minds are to be permitted freely to seek for it and are given free access to the results of others' search? That this freedom should be extended to men as of right is the fundamental claim of Mill's famous *Essay on Liberty*. It is only, he maintained, if you permit an opinion to be questioned and disputed from every point of view, that you are entitled to regard it as true, for it is only if all opinions are freely expressed and freely criticised that men will have a chance of discovering where the truth lies. Hence Mill's famous conclusion:

"If all mankind minus one were of one opinion, and only one person were of the contrary opinion, mankind would be no more justified in silencing that one person, than he, if he had the power, would be justified in silencing mankind."

Now if you believe that human beings have the power of recognising the truth, then you must also believe that, given the opportunity, sooner or later they will exercise it; that truth, in fact, like murder, will "out", if it is given half a chance.

The Evils that have Passed from Man's Life

Reflect for a moment—and as the moment is a black one, it will do us no harm to reflect—upon the evils that have disappeared from the life of man—witchcraft and cholera, slavery and gladiatorial games, duelling and torture.[1] Each of these evils must, at the time of its prevalence, have seemed, as war seems to-day, to be irremediable. Human nature being what it is, you could not, men must have said —men did in fact say—abolish slavery. But you did. How was the change effected? By reiterated appeals to men's sense of justice, to their compassion, above all to their reason. It was so obviously silly, said the opponents of duelling, to suppose that when you had a quarrel with somebody, the best way of showing yourself to be in the right was to make a hole with a pointed piece of metal in his body. And presently men saw that it *was* silly and duelling was abolished.

And the inference? That human beings really are reasonable. If they are suffering from some palpable evil, and if they can be shown how the evil may be prevented, then when the evil has continued long enough and they have suffered badly enough, they can be induced to take the steps that are necessary to end it.

2. FREEDOM AS A CONDITION OF GOODNESS

Most of us would agree that the goodness, such as it is, that accrues from the keeping of conventions is not worth the name. Nobody, for example, would account the fact

[1] When I was growing up the word "torture" could have been included without reservation, but to-day the assertion that it has disappeared must carry with it a reservation in regard to the practice of totalitarian States during the last twenty years.

that I refrain from cannibalism and human sacrifice to my moral credit. These things are not done in my society and I have no temptation to do them. A schoolboy who is forced to get up early, learn his lessons and eat only one helping of pudding because he is not given the chance of a second, gets no moral marks for early rising, diligence, or moderation at table. Goodness, in other words, if it is to be *really* goodness and not merely conventional behaviour must be freely acquired; it cannot be imposed from without by discipline, and it cannot be achieved by merely keeping the rules. You can make laws by Act of Parliament and you can make men obey your laws by force: but you cannot make men good by Act of Parliament and you cannot make them good by force. Goodness is something which can only be achieved by oneself. Goodness, then, demands that we should be free; free, if we have the insight to distinguish right from wrong, free, if we have the will to do the right and eschew the wrong; for, if you are forced to do your duty, it is no longer your duty that you do. The fact that goodness entails that we should be free to go right, means also that we must be free to go wrong, which is, of course, precisely the way we usually do go. But it is better to be free to go wrong and to take advantage of our freedom than to be forced to go right.

3. Freedom as a Condition of Art

Freedom is also a condition of the creation of what is beautiful in art and of what is valuable in literature. "They tell me that we have no literature now in France. I will speak to the Minister of the Interior about it." The remark, Napoleon's, throws into high relief the absurdity of trying to command beauty. If liberty is the air, the arts are the flowers of the spirit. Like flowers they can bloom only in a favourable environment, an environment which permits the spirit to blow where it listeth. It is perhaps unfortunate that they cannot be made to bloom by Act of Parliament; it is none the less true. You can no more cultivate the spirit of man by legislative enactment than you can break it by persecution. You can threaten to punish a poet if he does not turn out a sonnet a week, and you will get your sonnets. But as the melancholy record of official literature has shown, you will not get good sonnets. Hence when men's minds are required to march in step and their imaginations to function to order, art may be expected to go into retirement; and this, as history frequently demonstrates, is precisely what it does.

FREEDOM A NECESSITY OF THE GOOD LIFE

I have tried to show that in order that man may grow to his full stature, in order that he may achieve a society which is not beastlike but civilized, he must be free, free to think, free to act, free to create. Freedom is like health or air, something that we miss only in its absence. But its denial is a denial of all that makes life worth living, so that the spirit of the prisoner cries out for liberty and again for liberty, as the lungs of the man who is choking cry out for air. Liberty, indeed, is the air of the spirit.

II. The Free Man and the State

If I am right in thinking that freedom is a condition of the development of whatever things in human beings are valuable, what should be the relation to this freedom of the State? States we must have, if only because man, as

Aristotle once said, is a "Justice-needing animal", and "Justice needs the State". Needing justice, we need law to administer justice, and the law must, it is obvious, be enforced. There must, therefore, be somewhere a repository of force in the community, which is to say that there must be government and a State. What, then, should be the relation of the State, armed, as it must be, with the power of compulsion, to that free activity of human beings which is the source of all that is valuable in human life? This question divides itself into two. First, what *has been* the relation of the State to the free activity of civilized individuals? Secondly, what *ought* it to be?

1. What Has Been the Attitude of the State to the Free Mind?

The relation of States to the free activity of the human mind has been only too often one of disapproval, culminating in suppression. Distrusting originality and suspicious of novelty, authority habitually denounces the genius and discourages the inventor.

Take, for example, the official reception of novelty in science. There is scarcely an invention which has improved the lot of man that has not had to make its way in the teeth of the opposition of authority. Read of the struggles of Pasteur to win acceptance of the germ theory of disease —how, it was asked, could you cure diseases by looking through microscopes? Read—you can do so in Arnold Bennett's play, *Milestones*—of the derisive scepticism which greeted those who advocated iron ships—how, it was asked, could pieces of iron be expected to float? Read of the storm of ridicule which descended upon the originators of the telephone—the young men who invented this accepted amenity of human life came near starvation before they could persuade business men to put up enough money to take out a patent and float a company—and, as you read, you cannot but realise how inevitable and how violent is the opposition of the vested and the established to what is new, and shocking *because* it is new.

A similar reception has been accorded to novelty in art or morals. While officially sponsored art has been noteworthy for nothing but its mediocrity, new developments have almost invariably been regarded with horror and denounced as outrageous offences against the laws of harmony and perspective and the canons of taste.

In morals the State's concern is limited to ensuring that its citizens should observe the official code. I do not wish to decry the official code; far from it. But nobody would maintain that its observation, though it may be necessary, is sufficient for virtue. The fact that I keep the law, and refrain from stealing, murder, arson and incest, does not mean that I am a good man. It means merely that I refrain from those forms of vice which will get me into trouble with the law. There are, as we should all of us recognise, levels of morality beyond the law, so that a man may be a brutal bully, a woman may turn her home into a little hell of scolding, grudging and jealous fault-finding, an employer may exploit the economic helplessness of his men by extorting from them the last ounce of work for the least penny of pay, and not only remain on the right side of the law, but rise high in the esteem of the community. None of these is by any moral standard virtuous, yet each conforms to the requirements of the social code, and the State is satisfied. The State, in short, is not concerned that its citizens should be good; it is enough that they should keep the law.

2. WHAT SHOULD BE THE ATTITUDE OF THE STATE TO THE FREE MAN?

Let us suppose that I am right in thinking that the distinctive ends and purposes of man can be summed up under the search for knowledge, the pursuit of goodness and the cultivation of beauty. Then clearly it is the function of the State to assist men to pursue these, their distinctive purposes, and, so doing, to realise their natures. How can it perform this function?

First negatively, by providing that minimum background of security and stability in which alone the mind can develop, the spirit freely express itself. The philosopher cannot philosophise while the burglar is running off with his spoons, or the musician compose while his next door neighbour is abducting his wife. Thus the existence of a certain minimum background of order and security, the maintenance of a minimum level of decent behaviour by all the members of a society are conditions of the pursuit of the good life by any. It is the business of society to maintain this background.

THE STATE'S POSITIVE DUTY TOWARDS ITS CITIZENS

(a) *To Train their Minds.* But the State has another and a more positive function. It is not enough that it should maintain the conditions in which alone its citizens can lead what I have called the good life; it is necessary that it should equip them to lead it. The equipment is of two kinds. First, there is equipment of the mind. Citizens should be so trained that not only can they read, write and cypher, for these accomplishments are after all not so much education as the necessary means through which education can be achieved, but that they can if they so desire it, educate themselves. It is important not that men should be taught what to think, but that they should be taught how; important not that they should be taught what to read, but how to choose and criticise their reading; important not that they should be given information, but that their intelligence should be so trained that they can sift and value for themselves the information that they are given.

Education, in fact, has two functions. The first is to provide the citizen with a trained and critical intelligence, so that he can judge for himself what is good and bad, worthwhile and worthless. This requirement is of special importance in a democracy which demands of its citizens an alert and critical interest in public affairs. The second is to put a man in touch with the thought of abler minds than his own, and to make him acquainted with what great men have thought and said memorably about life. Only if a man be so equipped, can he play a free man's part in the affairs of a free community; only if he be so equipped, can he develop his faculties, enlarge his knowledge and cultivate his taste.

(b) *To Provide for their Bodies.* Secondly, there is the equipment of the body. A man who is over-worked and underfed, a man who goes in daily fear of losing his job, a man whose spirit is deadened and whose mind is dulled by the infinite repetition of the same mechanical process, above all a man who is hungry, cannot, it is obvious, develop the characteristics which I have maintained to be distinctive of our species. If in this pamphlet I have spoken but little of questions of bread and butter, it is because its theme is civilization and I take it for granted that their solution, though not a part, is a necessary condition of civilization. All the civilizations that have hitherto existed have been the close preserves of small leisured classes. In the past there was some sort of justification for this inequity; somebody, after all, had to do the dirty work of society. To-day, when machines have taken the place of serfs and slaves, there is no reason why civilized living should not be brought within the reach of all. But I think I can see a reason why it will not be so brought, until we collectively own and organise our economic resources. Accordingly, I am a socialist, believing that the community as a whole should own the means by which goods are produced and distributed, and should organise production and distribution in the interests of all its citizens.

The State, then, has the functions of educating the minds, of providing for the economic well-being of its citizens, and of establishing the conditions of order and security in which alone they can live what I have called the good life.

What the State Should Not Do

But in the modern world it has become important to emphasise not what the State should do, but what it should not do. I have said that it should seek to promote the good life by equipping its citizens to live it; it should seek to *promote,* but emphatically it should not seek to *prescribe.* Yet to prescribe is precisely what States in the modern world insist upon doing. There seem to me to be two reasons why those who care for the development of men and women and the preservation of civilization should resist the attempt of the State to enter the foreground of their lives, and to lay down for them what the good life should be.

First, there is not one good life for men, but there are many. People's native talents are different, and in developing them to their full extent they develop into different men and women, one man becoming a mathematician and another a doctor; one man expressing his creative vision in art, another contributing to the common happiness by the charm of his personality or to the common good by the selflessness of ungrudging service. Society, it has often been said, is like a living organism. Let us agree that in one sense at least it is; then we must also agree that the more complex the organism, the more diverse its parts and the more varied its components, the greater its value. A man, with his blood and his bones, his nerves and his sinews, his glands, his hair, his eyes, his ears, is a more admirable, because a more complex, organism than a jellyfish.

Now if the State is to tell men how they are to live, what they are to do, and what not to do, what they are to admire and what dislike, what beliefs they are to hold and what beliefs to denounce, variety will disappear. No doubt citizens who have been ironed and disciplined will be easier to govern; it is obviously easier to govern sheep than men. But what is the point of a well-governed society if in the process of achieving efficient government, the society loses all the values that make it worth governing?

Secondly, the only kind of good that the State can prescribe is the worship of itself, and of a man, the Dictator, who claims to be the expression of itself. Now those who worship the State must of necessity adopt its standards, share its desires, and cultivate its values. What, then, are the standards, the desires, and the values of States? Broadly speaking, they are such as are comprised in the notions of wealth and power. Throughout history States have sought to exercise power over other States, to conquer and to humiliate subject peoples, and to exploit propertyless classes. States acquire empires, claim sacred rights, and are the bearers of historic missions, in the course of pursuing which they find themselves embroiled with other States with the result that we get war.

Author's Confession of Faith

For my part, I repudiate these goods; it is not power, glory, strength, wealth and prestige that seem to me to be admirable, but such goods as I have described, the free activity of the human mind, the increase of moral virtue, the cultivation of good taste and skill in the art of living. But these are the goods not of States but of individuals, and those upon whom the State presumes to impose *its* conception of the good life are forced to forgo the latter goods, which are the goods of individuals, and accept the former, which are the goods of the State.

Men of my tradition in politics [1] are often accused of not loving their country: the accusation is untrue. I love England as much, I hope, as any man, but the England I love is not an imperial power with its far-flung possessions, but an island "set in a silver sea", a green island adorned by nature at her most gracious and her most beautiful, inhabited by kindly people, unassuming, modest and good-humoured, and tolerantly ready to put up with the ec-

[1] I shall try to say on a later page what this tradition is (see p. 187).

centricities of such men as myself. In a word, it is a little England and not a big Empire.

Conclusion on the State and the Individual

I conclude this account of the relation of the State to the individual by asking two questions. First, what is the individual? An expression of the State's will? A cell in a living organism? A drop of blood in an ocean of racial purity? A cog in a proletarian machine? An insect in a social ant heap, with no end or purpose save that of contributing to the well-being of the heap to which he belongs? There are many in Europe to-day who are prepared to answer that he is each and all of these, affirming that only the State is important and that the individual has no function except to serve the interests of the State. For my part, I would affirm that the individual is an end in himself, with a right to happiness in this world and a chance of immortality in the next, and that no end of the State, neither power nor glory nor sacred rights nor historic missions, can count in the balance against this right. Though I may have my doubts as to the immortality, I have none as to the importance of individuals. Souls are souls even if their life here is transitory, and though they may not be immortal, it is none the less the business of the government to treat them as if they were. The announcement of the importance of the individual is, in my view, the great gift of Christianity to the world.

Secondly, what is the State? The State, if I am right, was made by men for men to minister to their purposes and to serve their ends; it is a nuisance, but a necessary nuisance. But this necessary nuisance has been made by the Nazis into an idol which has become one of the greatest menaces to the happiness not only of the Germans themselves, but of civilized men the whole world over. Like the gods of old, the Nazi State is jealous and revengeful. To it belong the energies, the desires, the very lives of its citizens. It is the god; the officers of the Army and the Air Force are its high priests; the people its sacrifice. To this idol all that is individual and free and various in Germany has been sacrificed. Upon its young men it imposes a training whose sole object is to enable them to achieve efficiency in the art of slaughtering young men who are the citizens of other States, while it conceives of its welfare as something that can be secured only by inflicting horrible sacrifices upon its own citizens, in order that it may harm those of its alleged enemies. Yet in spite of its power and prestige the Nazi State is a monster owning no reality except by virtue of men's belief in it. There is in fact no political reality except in the individual, and no good for the State other than the good of the living men and women who call themselves its citizens. It is against the Nazi conception of man as made for the State that we are fighting to-day.

III. Conclusions: The War and Civilization

I have always been a pacifist—I hope the avowal will not set the reader against me. My reasons were different from those of many pacifists. I do not, for example, believe in the sacredness of human life. Whether life is a good thing or not, we do not know; for since we do not know what it is like not to be alive, we have nothing other than life with which to compare life.

If I saw a man laying a mine on a railway line just before an express train was due, I should have no hesitation in shooting him, just as I should have no hesitation in shooting a mad dog.

Again, I do not believe that the use of force is always wrong. I believe that it is sometimes necessary. If I saw a boy torturing a kitten, I should not hesitate to stop him with whatever force I could command. Similarly, I would use force to restrain a gangster and a thug simply because, unrestrained, their activities would render civilized behaviour and secure living impossible for those of us who are neither gangsters nor thugs. I recognise, then, that the State must be equipped with force and must be prepared to use it. And not only against gangsters and thugs! There are spheres of conduct in regard to which it does not in the least matter what people do, but it does matter enormously that they should all do the same thing. For example, it does not matter in the eye of God or the judgment of man whether the traffic goes to the left of the road or to the right; but it does matter enormously that, if the rule is that it goes to the left, the rule should be universally kept.

Never having objected on principle to the use of force, I had no difficulty as a pacifist in answering the historic question, "What would you do if you saw a German coming at your wife, mother, daughter, sister, cousin, aunt, or what-not with intent to rape her?" My answer was that I should quite certainly try to stop him with whatever means were at my disposal, and with whatever means were at my disposal I should, in similar circumstances, try to defend myself. Just as I would have equipped the government with force to restrain the gangster and the thug, so I would have equipped an international government with force to restrain a gangster nation. Hence so long as the

League looked like the first sketch of a world government, I was an ardent supporter of the League.

The Author's Pacifism. What It Was

Upon what, then, was my pacifism based? What was the ground for an opposition to war so wholehearted that there was never a time during the twenty years since the armistice when I was not engaged more or less actively in pacifist propaganda, speaking in and out of season against war and judging every turn of foreign, every development of home policy by the one standard of whether it seemed to render another war more likely or less? The ground was quite simply that war, as it seemed to me, blunted the faculties, impeded the activities and destroyed the goods that were distinctive of man and rendered the values of civilization unattainable.

It was not merely that war was savage and cruel; that it entailed physical agony in its grossest form for thousands of human beings; that it parted men from those who loved them and those whom they loved; that it used the bright talents of man for destruction; that it dulled and stupefied his spirit with boredom and brutalised it with violence. Upon all this, true enough as it is, I do not wish to dilate, for all this has to-day become as familiar as it is true. There are few of us to-day who have illusions as to the nature of war.

But though this and much more of the same kind may be laid to the account of the indictment of war, it was not the indictment that I principally wished to bring. To me it was the suspension of the activity of the free mind—in wars for liberty, liberty of thought is invariably one of the

first casualties; it was the palpable decline in human goodness—in wartime all the distinctively Christian virtues,
gentleness, compassion and love, are decried as surely as
their opposites, ferocity, hatred and malice are encouraged; it was the triumph of vulgarity, the lowering of
public taste, the degradation of art and literature, that war
entailed which seemed to me to constitute the main counts
in the case against it. In wartime all those characteristics
that I have defined as distinctively human fade and fail; in
order that they may win, men forget and forgo the qualities that confer upon them their distinctive humanity.

War inflames the spirit, clouds the mind, breeds hatred
in the heart, and pervades the very air we breathe with
panic and anger. Men go to war to preserve the way of
life that I have called civilized. They fight, as they say,
for ideals, for liberty and democracy, for justice to small
nations, for the right to live and to let live; but when the
war is over, it is found that the passions which it had been
necessary to arouse in order to win the war colour the
peace that ends it. Now a peace that expresses the hatred
and anger in the hearts of its makers cannot but betray
the ideals that led them to take up the sword.

And so I concluded that though wars might achieve results which others hold to be desirable, although they
might extend territory, increase dominion, humble rivals,
and enhance the power and prestige of empires, although
they might and did bring position and wealth to individuals, their effects upon the things that I hold to be desirable were almost uniformly disastrous. Hence it was because wars. whether they were won or lost, imperilled the
freedom of the mind, diminished virtue, made men blind
and deaf to beauty, and drove out of court all the varied
activities of civilized living, that I have called myself a

pacifist. Whatever gains might be achieved by war, these, I felt, were outweighed by the losses; for the gains were of matter, the losses were of the spirit; the gains were to the State, the losses were to individuals. Taking this view, I worked consistently for peace up to the very outbreak of war. Hating it and hating the betrayal of the Czechs, I nevertheless supported Munich, thinking that even such a settlement was better than a European war. In September, I believed that peace could have been preserved by the calling of a European conference, and when in November Hitler and Stalin launched their so-called peace offer, I maintained that it should have been welcomed and used as the basis for negotiation. I admitted that the negotiations might break down or that the peace offer might prove abortive. But even if the negotiations *did* break down, or even if peace were made and then, because of the perfidy of the Nazis, proved impossible to maintain, still, I thought, we ought to go to the uttermost length in accepting every possible chance of restoring peace. If the worst came to the worst, the war could always be "called on" again. Meanwhile, every day on which human beings were not devoting all their energies to slaughtering one another was, it seemed to me, a day gained. Moreover, if a halt could once be called to the killing, the halt, I thought, might well become permanent. Such was my mood up to the spring of this year.

This mood entailed, it was obvious, the suppression of much that I was feeling and would like to have expressed. I was not blind to the nature of the Nazi regime. At first, I could not credit what I heard; but as the years passed, and it seemed no longer possible to doubt the horror that was happening in Germany, it was with increasing difficulty that I kept silent. It was hard, indeed, to contain one's indignation, hard not to denounce this terrible thing that had reared its brazen front of violence and hate in the middle of the continent of Europe. Yet because of my hatred of war I kept silent, tried to understand from what causes the Nazi mentality had arisen, tried to persuade myself that if the causes were removed, the mentality might disappear. Treat it generously and the Nazi regime might, I maintained, become milder, might even mellow into a dictatorship which was at least tolerable.

The Issue Now Victory or Defeat

This mood belongs now to the past. War has been joined, and as the emotional temperature has risen, the possibility of a negotiated peace has vanished. There seems nothing for it, but to fight on until one side or the other is victorious. Faced by this situation, I am bound to ask myself which side I want to win. To this question there can be only one answer. It is not merely that, like the rest of us, I have an instinct to rally to the herd when the herd is in danger, that I too love England, and that the thought of the English countryside overrun fills the heart with a sick dismay; more important for my present purpose, because more pertinent to the theme of this pamphlet, is the realisation of what a Nazi victory would involve. In one way I am glad that things have reached a pass at which one can at last feel justified in speaking one's mind about the Nazi regime; in denouncing it for the evil thing one knows it to be. I have represented war as imperilling and diminishing the things that I hold to be valuable; I still do not doubt that this is, indeed, its effect. But if their continued existence is menaced by war, their destruction is certain in defeat. If we win this war, there is at least a chance that the mistakes of Versailles may be avoided and Europe given a generous peace, a peace which does not sow the seeds of future wars. There is also a chance—and here, of course, I speak only for myself—that those who share my opinions, subscribe to my values and wish them to be preserved may not wholly be without influence upon the making of the peace. But if the Nazis win, Western civilization, as I understand it, will be certainly destroyed.

The Nazi Regime

The Nazi regime is the eclipse of the mind, the death of the spirit and the Dark Night of the soul, the greatest single setback for humanity that history records. If there is ever again to be good and secure living, if civilized ways of thinking and behaving are ever to be restored to us, this horrible rule of gangsters and thugs must be overthrown.

In this pamphlet I have sought to represent as our chief good upon earth the development of those qualities which separate man from the beasts, and the pursuit of those values which only man can conceive. I have praised the activity of the free mind, the freedom of the moral will, the cultivation of the sense of beauty, the refinement of the spirit and the amenities of civilized living. I have argued that education should aim not at instilling the conclusions of other men, but the ability to reach conclusions for oneself; I have urged that society should be tolerant of and receptive to originality in art and morals; I have maintained that not society is valuable, but the men and women who compose it and that the function of the State should be limited to that of providing a background for the good life of its citizens. Freedom, tolerance, reasonableness, good taste, kindliness and compassion, the original activity of the mind, the right of expression and criticism, and the blossoming of the spirit in creative art—these are the articles of my creed, and these are also the essentials of civilization. Every single one of these the Nazis decry.

I will take one illustration from each of the three spheres of value which I have sought to praise. First, in the sphere of thought: here is a regime which has dishonoured all that is best in the German people; it has exorcized culture, burnt books, exiled artists, scientists, writers and philosophers, and made war upon the mind of man. Under its influence the great intellectual gifts of Germans have been devoted to the achievement of efficiency in the arts of slaughter, and to the contrivance of ever more ingenious and more sweeping methods of destruction. Is it any wonder that when war came, the Germans should possess an advantage in the ability to slaughter over their adversaries the Allies, whose intellectual faculties have been otherwise engaged, whose preoccupations have been different?

Secondly, in the sphere of morals: here is a regime which glories in brutality, uses cruelty as a method of government and lies as an instrument of policy. Compassion, mercy, consideration for the helpless, tolerance and tenderness, all these it proclaims to be decadent and seeks to eradicate.

In the sphere of art, the vision of the creative spirit is denied and the artist is tied to the chariot wheels of the State which degrades his art into an instrument of propaganda. "So long as there remains in Germany any neutral or non-political art," Goebbels has declared, "our task is not ended."

Freedom in Germany

Finally, there is freedom, freedom which, as I have tried to show, is the condition of the realisation of all civilized goods. Freedom in Germany has been destroyed. The Nazi government gags its people; it taps telephones and opens letters; it sets spies and eavesdroppers to over-hear and report upon the most casual conversation; it plants its secret police and their creatures in cafés, restaurants, shops and even private households to arrest its citizens and imprison them without trial, or after a trial in a party court for offences hitherto unknown to any code of law; it toils and tortures its intellectuals to death in concentration camps; it forces its unfortunate victims to suppress at every moment the normal workings of the human intellect and the natural pulsations of the human heart. Under this regime everybody must do and think as their rulers bid them, under pain of the most savage penalties if they refuse. And what do their rulers bid them? To denounce freedom and glorify oppression, to hate peace and to praise war, to renounce truth and to worship lies. It is because these things constitute the denial of civilization that, if civilization is to survive, the Nazis must be beaten. A Nazi victory would usher in a new Dark Age for Europe, an age in which the mind of man would go into prison and the spirit of man into retreat. If civilization survived at all, it would survive in holes and corners in daily peril of its existence. Perhaps there would be retreats in which men would gather to keep alive something of the old values and the old culture, as the monks kept alive the remnants of the Græco-Roman civilization after the invasion of the barbarians and the sack of Rome. But such retreats cannot, I submit, establish themselves in a continent dominated by the Nazis.

THE CONSEQUENCES OF DEFEAT

For the defeat of the Allies in this war would bring consequences very different from those which have attended the defeat of nations in other wars. In previous wars a defeated nation has lost territory, has been mulcted of a heavy indemnity, has been shorn of power and robbed of prestige; but there has been no serious interference with its people's way of life. Thus the defeats of France in 1815 and again in 1870 were the prelude to the most active periods of French civilization. Anxious to forget the sufferings and disasters of war, Frenchmen turned to the cultivation of the mind and the spirit. But a Nazi victory would not permit such cultivation. A Nazi victory would deprive us of our empire, rob us of our wealth, take from us our economic controls, and lower our standards of living. But this is not all, and it is not the worst. If the Nazis won this war, they would establish in England a puppet government supported by a servile parliament; they would control the Press; they would censor books and periodicals; they would enslave the working class, depriving them of those rights and safeguards against exploitation which have been won during a hundred and fifty years of struggle. The liberties of our democracy, that a man should not be imprisoned without a trial, that he should be tried by a jury of his peers, that he should be sentenced by an impartial judiciary, that he should make the laws through his representatives elected by secret ballot—in a word the whole body of democratic forms and institutions for which our fathers struggled so hard and so long and at last established, all would disappear from England as utterly and, it may be, as irretrievably as they have already disappeared from Germany. This, then, is veritably a war for civilization.

THE RIGHTS OF MAN

By

HAROLD J. LASKI

THE RIGHTS OF MAN

I

FOR something like a century and a half it has been the central purpose of Western civilisation to find the secret of combining individual freedom with social order. The fulfilment of that purpose has been achieved in different ways, and in different degrees; there has been one method in France and another in Great Britain. But it is an aim the fulfilment of which has been generally and increasingly desired wherever there has been respect for human personality.

Because this is the case, during the last century and a half men have striven consistently to limit all privilege, whether it was built upon birth or creed or race. They have battled to impose upon governments the duty to avoid arbitrary action, to rule in terms of law and not in terms of discretion. They have claimed the right for ordinary people to choose the governments by which they will be ruled. That is why, after long struggles, free and equal suffrage has been established. That is why, also, the common man has been given the opportunity, at stated intervals, to change the persons by whom he has been governed, if he so desires. Before the war of 1914, it was widely regarded as one of the supreme triumphs of civilisation that government should be based upon free discussion and that minority opinion should have the right to win political power by persuasion.

The Independence of Justice

Parallel with his growing fulfilment was the recognition that each member of the community had a right to citizenship in the fullest sense of the term. He was entitled to voice his grievances; he could organise, with his fellow-citizens, to obtain redress for them. He was not to be penalised for doing so unless the manner of his protest threatened social peace. To secure him in these liberties, civilised States developed, with an increasing sense of its importance, the great principle inherent in the English writ of habeas corpus. It is the principle that no man should legally suffer penalties unless it could be shown by evidence before independent judges that he had broken a specific law. This principle was felt to be the very essence of individual freedom; and it was because it was so regarded that the most careful steps have been taken, in every democratic State, to safeguard the independence of the judges. Neither king nor prime minister, neither parliament nor civil servant, could interfere with the judge's performance of his task. Here was the secret which prevented the development of tyranny in our rulers.

Constitutional Government

The right to help in the choice of those by whom he was to be governed; the right, at stated intervals, to refuse the re-appointment to office of those who operated the power of the State; these were of the essence of that constitutional government which, as England discovered in the seventeenth century, made change compatible with peace. From England, in the eighteenth century, the doctrine spread to America and the Continent of Europe; after 1789, its acceptance became the ambition of every State which recognised that necessary social adaptation could not otherwise be peacefully achieved, and to make those rights effective, it was increasingly realised that constitutional government could not be maintained unless there were (i) freedom of expression and (ii) freedom of association. For if men are penalised when they speak and organise freely, that utterance and organisation are alone likely which please those who sit in the seats of power; and sooner or later, they will suppress all whose speech and action they find inconvenient. History confirmed the experience that the narrower the numbers of those to whom the rights of man were conceded, the smaller would be the number of those to whom a share in the benefits of social organisation was possible. It is not accident that the wider the area of citizens to which a government has been compelled to appeal, the wider has been both the extent and intensity of its response to their wants.

There is nothing mysterious in these principles. They were wrested, after infinite effort and profound suffering, from a society in which the claims of the many were sacrificed to the privileges of the few. No doubt their realisation has been both slow and incomplete. Yet it is difficult to compare the results of their operation in States which have adopted them with the results in States from which they have been absent without a profound sense of the importance they have had for the dignity and happiness of the common man. For it is out of them that the workers have been able to build their trade unions and the co-operative movement. It is out of them, also, that political parties, like the Labour Party in Britain, which, a hundred years ago, would pretty certainly have been denied a legal existence, have now become not merely an element in the national life, but the vital alternative to the government in power. Out of them, too, has come the inestimable benefit of religious toleration; no State which lives by these principles seeks to discriminate against the private faith a man may choose to hold, or his right, if he so desire, to have no faith at all. And it is out of them, further, that, above all in the last forty years, the negative State has been transformed into the positive State.

A Century Ago

That phrase deserves some annotation, not least in a British context. The citizen of this country who was born after 1906 can hardly realise the rights he enjoys compared with those at the disposal of his predecessor who was born during the Napoleonic wars. There was no national educational system a century ago; if a primitive factory legislation existed, until 1844 there was no means of its effective enforcement. There were no workmen's compensation, no trade boards, no serious local self-government, no public health services of any kind. What industrial conditions were like can be read in the grim pages of Dickens' *Hard Times,* or the remorseless analysis of Engels' *Condition of the English Working Class of 1844.* Trade unions were still illegal; and even after the repeal of the Combination Acts in 1825, their status was at the mercy of a prejudiced bench. Public libraries were a vague dream in a few scattered minds. Unemployment and health insurance were undreamed of: neither locally nor centrally did a competent civil service exist. Typhus and cholera still raged in the great towns. The enfranchisement of the masses was dreaded by an aristocracy which controlled at least a third

of the seats in the House of Commons and was the major
part of every cabinet. Newspapers were few, and so expensive that even those who could read could hardly afford
them unless their situation was comparatively comfortable.
The standard of living was, at best, one-quarter of what it
is to-day. Maternity and child welfare were unknown.
The "condition of England" question did not, until the
time of Robert Owen and the Chartist movement, make
any serious impact upon the mind of that generation. The
notion that a working man had the right to state his case
in the House of Commons would have been regarded as
an outrage by even the most advanced members of the
leading political parties of the day.

The Popular Will

The change from a negative to a positive State is the
history, slow, it is true, but sure, of the deliberate use of
the power of the State to mitigate the consequences of
social inequality. It was a change which came piece by
piece; but what is significant in its coming was the fact
that it was always a response made by the political party
in power to the demands of the working-class voter to
share in the gain as well as in the toil of living. He wanted
to see his needs translated into terms of statute; and because he exercised an increasingly active political power,
he had the right to compel that response. But that right
would have been meaningless unless he could call for the
support of an active body of citizens, able to say what they
wanted, accustomed to organise, and capable of protecting
their power to convince others that they were entitled to
secure the satisfaction of their claims. The condition, in a
word, of social progress was the increasing acceptance of

the rights of man, the recognition that these inhered in him as a citizen regardless of class or creed or race. The rights of man meant, and were understood increasingly to mean, that the popular will, and only the popular will, was the effective source of power.

The Tyrant's Will

It is not necessary to deny the inadequate fulfilment of all that this development has made possible to recognise that upon the conception it embodies the whole fulfilment of personality depends. For once the conception is denied that it is the obligation of all governments to respect these rights, that their claim to obedience rests upon that respect, it follows at once that citizens are transformed from persons with the right to be consulted, with the opportunity, therefore, of influence, into persons with no prospect of influence and no function save the duty passively to accept the orders that are issued to them by government.

There is no place then in the State for consent; power is bound to rest upon naked coercion. All criticism becomes proof of ill-will; all opposition is transformed into conspiracy. The only means, in such an atmosphere, that the government can have of knowing the mind of its citizens is by espionage; and dependence upon such means involves, that it may retain its power, the suppression of all whom it is unable to coerce into active support. The symbols of its regime then become the secret police and the concentration camp. It is driven to coerce because it no longer feels able to persuade.

Having, therefore, made intolerance its central principle of action, it can no longer treat human beings as ends;

they become, inevitably, mere instruments of purposes upon which it has decided. They have no right to share in the making of those purposes; they are deprived of the opportunity to speak their minds about them. All that is demanded of them is the mentality of slaves; and every aspect of intellectual life is rigorously co-ordinated to produce that mentality. Order and obedience become the highest good; freedom is decried as an evil thing. The atmosphere, as always happens under dictatorship, breeds arrogance and cruelty in those who rule, servility and hypocrisy in those who obey. And because, as again always happens under a dictatorship, some compensation must be offered to a people for its slavery, conquest abroad is attempted to draw the mind of its subjects away from their misery and servitude at home. Over two thousand years ago, Aristotle, analysing the experience of that ancient world he knew so profoundly, remarked that the end of dictatorship is war. The tyrant cannot afford the luxury of peace; he requires the drama of external conflict to build his victims into that desperate unity which would otherwise be destroyed in civil war at home.

II

The Nazi System

This prologue is the background in which it is necessary to set the proper perspective of the Nazi system. The explanation of Hitler's rise to power is not a simple one. Partly, it was due to the frustrated nationalism which hungered for revenge after defeat in the War of 1914. Partly, also, it was the outcome of the grave economic crisis which previous German governments were unable to solve. Partly, again, it was due to the fact that constitutional government, which, in a full sense, was new in Germany, was associated with defeat and economic crisis; it paid the penalty for sins for which it had little responsibility save the lack of will to repress conspirators. Division among its friends, a propaganda of consistent lying, the formation of private armies condoned by high officials and financed by organised reaction, the use of violence against men too proud (or too weak) to retort in kind, even though they had the legal right and duty to repress it, the general misery of a population psychologically weary of endless political conflict resulting always in weak government, all these played their part. Something is due to mean intrigue, not a little to the faithless betrayal of his high office by President Hindenburg. The outcome of these complexities was the admission of Hitler to the Chancellorship of the German Reich in January 1933. The outcome of his accession to power was not merely the destruction of the rights of man. The outcome was the establishment of a regime which denies all validity to the conception of human rights. Its maker boasts openly that his only purpose is the predominance of the German State in Europe, and that everything must be sacrificed to securing that predominance.

The Nazi Method

The results are stark indeed. Let us set out in detail what has been done to this end and the methods by which it has been achieved.

1. No opposition to the government is permitted. All organisations, therefore, the principles of which are op-

posed to those of the government, are destroyed; all organisations, the members of which express, as individuals,
doubts of, or hostility to, the methods of the regime are
persecuted. There is, therefore, only one political party,
the Nazi Party; all others, without exception, have been
suppressed. The government and the Nazi Party are now
identical. There are no longer elections to the legislature.
Local self-government, in the British sense, has disappeared; in its stead, its destinies are entrusted to officials
appointed by, and responsible to, the Nazis. From time
to time a plebiscite approving Hitler's policies has been
taken. The fact that ninety-eight to ninety-nine per cent.
of the population has voted, and that all but a handful of
them have voted in his favour, is ample proof that the
voting is unfree when it is remembered that, in the last
free elections to the legislature, he did not obtain, as in a
free election he has never obtained, a majority there. The
legislature still meets occasionally to hear a pronounce-
ment from him. But it is immediately dismissed, and that
without the right of discussion, even though its members
have been hand-picked by the Nazi Party.

Labour

2. All the trade unions have been abolished. Workers
are organised into a "Labour Front", the main officials of
which are appointed by the Nazi Party. There is no right
to strike, and all industrial differences are settled by the
officials of the Labour Front, that is, by the government.
It is obviously a consequence of this that there has been
a serious decline in wages and that the hours of labour
have been considerably lengthened since the Nazis came
to power.

3. As the trade unions have gone, so also the co-operative movement has been destroyed as a free form of control by organised consumers. Its connection with similar democratic movements abroad has been sufficient to make it suspect to a party which will tolerate no criticism of its will.

Religion

4. Organised religion has been fiercely attacked by the government wherever it has failed to accept the aims of Nazism. Those who sought, in the Protestant churches, to render to Cæsar what was due to Cæsar and to God the things that are God's, have been cut off from financial support, forbidden to preach, to use the property of the Church, or to publish their opinions; in extreme cases of protest, they have been sent, like the famous Pastor Niemöller, to concentration camps. A pagan religion, under the patronage of Rosenberg, the "philosopher" of Nazism, has been encouraged. The Roman Catholic Church, despite a concordat between Hitler and the Holy See, has been even more severely treated. Its courageous refusal to accept the monstrous racial theories of the Nazis has led to what is called the "White" war against priests and nuns. Scandalous trials have been staged against them for currency violations and moral turpitude; and hundreds have been sent to prison and concentration camps. The leaders of the Nazi Party are openly contemptuous of Christianity, partly because its insistence on the universality of the rights of man is inconsistent with Nazi racial theory, and partly, no doubt, because they greatly covet the immense property of the Churches as a fund through which to cope with their financial difficulties.

Freedom of Thought

5. There is no longer any freedom of opinion in the German Reich. All newspapers, periodicals, books, plays, music, art, the wireless and the films are under the censorship of the notorious Dr. Goebbels, the Minister of Propaganda. Nothing can be published which is not approved by his Department, and the "line" to be taken by publications is indicated to their authors. No one, either, may be a journalist unless he is a member of the journalists' organisation, admission to which depends upon the Ministry's approval. Broadly speaking, therefore, the German people has no access to any information save what the Ministry of Propaganda approves. It is a serious offence to listen to foreign broadcasts. Much of the socialist and democratic literature of the past is now inaccessible to readers except by permission. Famous German writers of Jewish origin, like Heine, may no longer be quoted; and important works of modern scientists, like those, for instance, of Freud and Einstein, are officially banned, either because they are by Jews, or because their tendency is disapproved by the government.

Education

6. All forms of education have been strictly subordinated to Nazi purposes. Thousands of "unsound" teachers, i.e., teachers who were suspected of a lack of sympathy with Nazism, have been dismissed. The curriculum has been transformed so that the glorification of war and Nazi racial theories are now an essential element in it. From the earliest period, children are indoctrinated with the

worship of Hitler. They are even encouraged to report at school any criticisms of the regime they may hear at home. The purpose is to produce a well-regimented mass obedient to the discipline imposed from above. In the Universities, hundreds of the most eminent professors have been compelled to resign, and their places, only too often, have been taken by incompetent party hacks. Lists have even been compiled of names students may not cite in their doctoral theses; many of these—those, for instance, of Spinoza and Karl Marx—are recognised outside Nazi Germany as among the supreme names in our intellectual heritage. The German student, in short, is being made the prisoner of a narrow and imposed tradition, conformity with which is the condition of a successful career. It is not, therefore, remarkable that careful observers report a decline in the standards of all German Universities, even in the more technical subjects like medicine and the physical sciences.

Justice

7. It is the frank claim of Hitler that the law is simply the embodiment of his supreme will. In the service of this definition, the older independence of the courts has gone; gone, also, is the notion of fixed legal rules. "Law is what is useful to the German nation." In accordance with this view, all judicial officers not willing to act in this spirit have been removed from the Bench, and their places taken by party-members. Trials need no longer be held in public. Punishments are immensely more severe. It is even dangerous to defend those whom the government has decided to find guilty; the defender of Thälmann, the Communist leader, for example, was a distinguished ex-naval officer who, after 1918, took up the study of the law. For attempt-

ing to take the defence of his client with the proper seri-
ousness, he was sent to a concentration camp, whence he
escaped abroad. It is possible to be held for long periods
without trial. It is possible to be accused of one offence
and to be convicted, not on that ground, but because the
court holds that the accused's attitude is incompatible with
the well-being of the State. In the People's Court, a revo-
lutionary tribunal with the right to inflict the highest penalties, two of the three members are chosen from amongst
the Nazi Party "because of their special knowledge of the
defence against subversive activities, or because they are
most intimately connected with the political trends of the
nation". It is as though, in Britain, leading members of the
Conservative Party were to judge their opponents in political cases when a Conservative government was in office, and
leading members of the Labour Party to do the same for
their opponents when the Labour Party was in office. Obviously, under such circumstances, a fair trial is impossible.
And this impossibility is made even greater when the law
orders punishment for such vague offences as acts "deemed
in conflict with the healthy sentiment of the people" even
when no specific statute has been violated. Law, under the
Nazis, is degraded to the position of a mere instrument of
a political party.

Terror

8. But there is not merely the tragedy of this degradation of the law. The Nazi Party rules by terror, and its
weapons are the secret police and the concentration camp.
The activities of the former are endless. Its real business is
to prevent the growth of criticism and opposition in Germany. It opens private correspondence; it taps private tele-

phones; it installs dictaphones in private houses, even, it is alleged, in the embassies of Foreign Powers; it organises espionage through hired and voluntary informers; it uses *agents-provocateurs;* it even organises the kidnapping of enemies of the regime living abroad. It has the power of detention without trial, and literally scores of thousands of its victims, some, no doubt, guilty, but the overwhelming majority innocent of any offence, have been sent to concentration camps. There, as we know from incontrovertible evidence, terrorism is the normal order of the day. Men are beaten, tortured, starved, subjected to indescribable humiliations, often for no other offence than being a Jew, or having had "liberal" or socialist convictions. At least hundreds have died as the result of their treatment in these camps, many have committed suicide; many have been driven insane. Outright murder by the camp guards—often concealed under the fiction of "shot whilst trying to escape"—has not been infrequent.

The purpose of the system is to terrorise the masses into obedience; and the worst features of it have been employed against supporters of the regime whose loyalty has been for some reason suspected, not less than against its opponents. Jews and Communists have perhaps suffered most. But perhaps the most striking example of the Brown Terror was the infamous night of June 30, 1934, when Hitler and Göring were directly responsible, under hideous circumstances, for the assassination of some thousands of their own supporters, including some of the best-known members of the party, for alleged conspiracy. No proofs of that conspiracy have ever been produced; and Hitler's only justification for what was, in fact, simply a brutal massmurder was that on that June night he represented "the supreme embodiment of justice".

The Leader and the Race

9. Underlying these methods are two conceptions, neither of which can be termed intelligible to a British citizen. The first is the conception of the Führer (leader) as the incarnation, almost the Divine incarnation, of the German people, through whom its mission is to be fulfilled. The second, closely related to the first, is the conception of the German people as the embodiment of the highest racial values, the true State-builders, the essential pioneers in science and culture, the great creators of eternal works of art. The German race is the noblest of all races; its purity must be safeguarded at all costs. It is entitled to dominate all others; by so doing it gives to the world a higher culture than any inferior race can do. To preserve its purity, the German State is entitled to control all Germans who live under other States; it is thus the fulfilment of a racial obligation to bring Austria, Memel, Danzig and the Sudetenland under the power of Germany. That, also, is why German minorities living abroad, as in the South Tyrol and the Baltic States, must be repatriated to Germany; why, again, those Germans who continue to live abroad, as, for example, in the United States of America, owe their first allegiance to the German race, and hence to the German State which is its political expression.

To preserve "racial" purity, marriage between Germans, and certain "inferior" races is forbidden; and compulsory sterilisation may be imposed on persons in whom hereditary disease may injure the purity of the "race". Physicians are compelled by law to notify all such diseases to the health authorities. It is reliably asserted that over half-a-million persons have been sterilised on these grounds; and the code of domestic relations and of inheritance has been harshly revolutionised in the name of a supposed "racial science" that is adjudged worthless by every competent biologist in every country outside the Nazi realm. The whole conception is simply a fantastic notion of Hitler's, picked up by him from writers whose authority he was quite incompetent to judge, and imposed on the German people by him only because the law is simply his will and there is no one to say him nay.

The Jews

10. The most tragic aspect of this "racialism" is the results it has had upon the position of the Jews. Anti-Semitism is one of Hitler's cardinal beliefs, and he attributes all the ills of civilisation to the Jews. As soon as he came into power, their wholesale persecution began. They were rapidly eliminated from all public offices. They were denied the right to practise in any of the main professions. They could not write for the Press or act in the theatre. They were excluded from the Universities beyond one and one-half per cent. of the total student-body. They had to sit on special benches in the elementary schools. Marriage or sex-relations between Jews and Germans was made a crime. They were deprived of all civic rights. They cannot be members of the Labour Front. They are excluded from many towns, and from many areas and public buildings in other towns. Thousands of them have been sent to concentration-camps, for no offence but being born a Jew. Thousands more have been compelled to sell their businesses to non-Jewish Germans with heavy loss. Thousands, again (it is probable that the number is more than 150,000) have been driven into exile, often with the loss of everything they possess. The synagogues have been desecrated. Po-

groms have been frequent. Enormous fines have been imposed on the Jewish community in Germany.

The extreme agony of the persecution was reached on
January 1, 1939, when an ordinance prohibited any Jew
from the ownership or operation of any retail or wholesale business, or from the occupation of an independent
artisan; and all Jewish children were compelled to attend
special Jewish schools. Almost all avenues of employment,
in fact, are now closed to the Jew, and the choice before
him is that of emigration or starvation. The organ, indeed,
of the Hitler guard, wrote of these measures that the day
had now come when impoverished Jewry "would sink into
criminality and could be wiped out by fire and sword".
Yet when Hitler came to power in January 1933, the
whole Jewish community of Germany represented only
half a million citizens in a nation of over seventy millions.

Nothing like these infamies has been known in Europe
since the worst excesses of the Middle Ages. They have
been condemned by public opinion all over the world.
Great public figures, the Pope, the President of the United
States, the Prime Minister of Great Britain, have given
expression to their horror at these brutalities; President
Roosevelt, in November 1938, withdrew the American
Ambassador from Berlin as a protest against them.

As a campaign, it has been based upon accusations again
and again refuted, and no longer accepted by any rational
mind. Its explanation lies, probably, in three realms. In
part, it is the outcome of the pathological psychology of
Hitler himself; the depth of this is evident from his discussion of, indeed obsession with, the Jewish problem. In
part, it is the result of the need, inherent in any dictatorship built upon terror, to have an enemy to whom all
wrong can be attributed, and against whom victories may

be continually announced. In part, further, the persecution of the Jews has provided opportunities for satisfying Hitler's followers with the posts, in the professions and businesses, the Jews formerly occupied. But the whole world has realised how evil a thing it is to revive, as the considered practice of a government, barbaric intolerance from which, for centuries, humanity has been striving to rid itself. To accustom a nation to accept persecution as part of its way of life is to sap its moral foundations. The men who were trained and encouraged to destroy the Jews are the men who have gone on, by a natural sequence, to impose revolting cruelties on Czechs and Poles. Persecution becomes a habit which grows by what it feeds on.

The State Is All

11. Underlying all the strategy of the Nazi system there lies one central principle of the first importance: a complete contempt for the common man. The underlying assumption of the Nazi regime is the unimportance of the individual. In countless speeches and writings, Hitler and his chief followers have emphasised this view. The masses are made only to be led. They are plastic material to be moulded by the leader into any shape he pleases. They are not fit to exercise power; that is the business of a specially chosen governing class alone fit to preside over the destinies of the State. They are convinced that there is no limit to the degree in which the people can be deceived; its natural role is submission. In itself, it is ignorant and anarchic, and incapable of great actions save as it is dominated by the leader's will. Left to itself, the people is pacifist and materialist; it becomes capable of greatness

only as the leader subdues it to purposes he only can understand.

The Hitler Government, therefore, rejects all the democratic and liberal notions of Western civilisation. The individual has no rights, but only duties. He is not an end in himself, but the means to another end which the leader defines. His duty, therefore, is simply to obey the will of the State as that is shaped by the leader. It is treason to question it, it is a betrayal of the folk-spirit in which alone he can find his meaning. He must not criticise the findings of that spirit; to do so is to weaken it by a rationalism which, because it doubts, jeopardises the unity of the nation. To maintain that unity, to keep it ever more strong, is the highest task of the State. Beside it, the happiness of the ordinary man is nothing; his little purposes must give way to that supreme purpose.

It is upon this basis that the whole legislation and organisation of Nazi society has been built. Man is educated for the State; he lives and works for the State; woman, in her turn, is an instrument to breed children for the State. And in return, the individual can comfort himself with the knowledge that, as the State grows ever more strong, it becomes the dominating factor in the life of the world. What it wants, it takes. Whatever it wants, it is justified in taking since it is the organised expression of the people that is called to rule the world. To fulfil that mission everything is justified. The goodness of a treaty, the rightness of a war, the validity of domestic legislation, all these depend upon the single test of whether they lead to the fulfilment of the national mission. The leader is his people; his will is its law. Where he goes, it must follow, and he is always right. The only test of his actions is their success. He has the right to do whatever he has the power to achieve. His only sin is weakness.

III

The Western Ideal

No one can compare the way of life this outlook embodies with that of the civilisation to which we are accustomed in Britain without recognising at once that it is incompatible with all the major things we value. The last hundred years, at least, of our history have been the record of a continuous and persistent effort to break down the barriers of privilege in the interest of ordinary men and women; the seven years of the Nazi regime are the history of a deliberate and conscious effort to build up a new privileged class whose will alone is to count in the direction of the State. We have sought increasingly to realise equality before the law; the Nazi regime is a denial that this is legitimate. We have attempted to protect the individual in his civic capacity by insisting that his experience must be taken account of, that he may freely report it, that he may organise to make it effective; the Nazi philosophy starts by an insistence on the worthlessness of individual experience. We have given independence to our judges because there is no government we are prepared to trust to be at once prosecutor and judge in its own cause; the Nazis have made the judge the creature of the State and, even beyond that, have given the police an authority over citizens which may make thought itself a dangerous adventure. We have insisted that no government is fit to rule unless, at stated intervals, it has to justify its policy to those from which it has derived its power; the Nazi scheme con-

fers permanent authority upon Hitler and his followers
without any right in the people to judge of its results. Religious toleration, racial equality, the rights of each nation-
state to live its life in its own way, these principles we have
sought increasingly to make the basis of our national and
international policy; all of them are denied by those who
now shape the destinies of the Nazi State.

Greece and Christianity

In a broad way, the path which, until the advent of the
Nazis to power in Germany, Western civilisation as a
whole was seeking to follow was one which resulted from
the impact on our lives of the philosophies of Greece and
Christianity. Its keynote was the discovery of the infinite
worth of the individual human being, the insistence that
the justification of social institutions lay in their power to
evoke that worth and to give it the increasing chance of
fulfilment. Democracy and toleration were born of nearly
three thousand years' growing confidence in the validity
of this ideal. It was a confidence, be it added, increasingly
proven in human experience. We found that men excluded from a share in power were excluded, also, from
the benefits of power. We found that all governments
which were free from popular control inevitably tended
to degenerate. We found that the rule of one, or of a few,
bred arrogance and cruelty in those who exercised power,
and servility and brutishness in those who were its subjects. We found that, in every society, the more numerous
the citizens who shared in the active life of the State, the
more responsive did it prove to the wants they felt. We
found, perhaps above all, that the more profoundly we
could build the policy of the State upon the free consent

of its citizens, the greater was the moral self-respect they displayed. We could not regard the State as something different from its citizens. It found its fulfilment in their fulfilment, its success was their success. Its power lay in the happiness they achieved through its operations.

This is the central tradition of Western civilisation. For all its imperfections in realisation, it is the tradition to the fulfilment of which, in increasing measure, all modern history has contributed. It is, let it be noted, a tradition which all political parties have shared in common. Conservative and Socialist, Liberal and even Communist, Christian and Jew and Agnostic, may have differed about its realisation in method or in pace; about the validity of the large ends it has in view they have hardly differed at all. To make the common man the master of his own destiny; to recognise in democratic freedom the atmosphere in which that mastery can alone be attained; to insist that the attainment of democratic freedom means the admission of rights in the citizen which the State denies at its peril; these have been the accepted commonplaces of Western civilisation. However often they have been denied, in the long run they have always triumphed over their denial; and whenever they have been denied, the abuse of authority for ends incapable of national justification has always been the consequence. Those who have sought to resist their affirmation have seemed, as Edmund Burke once said, to resist the eternal principle of human dignity.

It is against this central tradition of Western civilisation that Nazism is in revolt. It seeks power for the sake of power. It is hostile to freedom, hostile to rights, hostile to the vital postulate of the infinite worth of human beings. What it cannot convince, it is prepared to coerce; what it cannot take by duplicity, as in the case of Prague, it is prepared to take by violence, as in the case of Warsaw. Because it refuses to admit the validity of any experience of which its leaders do not approve, it will persecute and destroy as it hacks its way to power. There is nothing new in Nazism; an old tyranny wears only a new mask. It is uglier than past tyrannies because it is better organised, more cruel because it is more efficient. But it raises an ancient question once again, even if more sharply and more poignantly than in any previous time.

The Evil Challenge

It is the question of whether the masses are to be free men with rights, or slaves without rights, who live therefore at the behest of others. Mankind has faced that challenge before; and answered it triumphantly. No doubt in the form in which it is made to-day it is more brutal and more menacing than any since the Reformation; rarely in the past have those who sought to subdue the world to their despotism boasted of the ugly methods by which they propose to fulfil their purpose. But it is natural that this should be the case. To put a whole people in chains, as the Nazis have put the German people in chains, has struck with horror all those who still cherish the traditions of our essential inheritance. To seek to make the whole world a prison of which the Nazi leaders are the jailers could only be accomplished by men to whom that tradition has ceased to have meaning. They are driven by the logic of their attitude to refuse to men those rights for which they have fought for over two thousand years. For those rights are incompatible with their power; they are intended to be the safeguards against their manner of its exercise. The Nazi leaders represent that ultimate corruption of the human spirit which pervades and infects every government which denies its responsibility to ordinary men. Like the Satan of Milton's great epic they have identified good with evil. In battling against the ends they seek to realise we are fighting to restore the authority of procedures upon which the whole quality of civilised life has been found to depend.

One final word may be said in defending, as in this war we are defending, the concept of the rights of man against the claims of naked power; we defend a cause as high as there is in the record of mankind. It will not be an easy victory; and its accomplishment on any showing will be attended with grave risks. The vital task before us is not merely to win; even more, it is to win by the method of freedom. The way to vindicate our rights against the challenge they have encountered is to make them everywhere more ample and more profound. The way to attack the principle of despotism is to make the principle of our democratic faith more living, that its hold upon the common man may be more profound. There is, on the experience of history, an active strength in the free consent of democratic peoples which has an endurance beyond the power of any tyranny to rival. The source of that strength is in the faith of the common man that those who govern him respect his rights and search for their enlargement in terms of his demands. Where faith can evoke that loyalty, a people can meet its challenge with confidence. It has those qualities of magnanimity and wisdom upon its side against which the "evil things" have never, in the long run, been able to prevail.